# Daily Devotions
## *with* Herman Bavinck
# Bavinck

# Other Devotional Works
# by Donald K. McKim

*Advent: A Calendar of Devotions 2017* (Abingdon, 2017)

*Breakfast with Barth: Daily Devotions* (Wipf & Stock, 2019)

*Coffee with Calvin: Daily Devotions*
(Westminster John Knox Press, 2013)

*Conversations with Calvin: Daily Devotions*
(Wipf & Stock, 2019)

*Everyday Prayer with John Calvin* (P&R, 2019)

*Everyday Prayer with the Reformers* (P&R, 2020)

*Everyday Prayer with the Puritans* (P&R, 2021)

*Following Faith with P. T. Forsyth: Daily Devotions*
(Cascade, 2022)

*Living into Lent* (Westminster John Knox Press, 2020)

*Moments with Martin Luther: 95 Daily Devotions*
(Westminster John Knox Press, 2016)

*Mornings with Bonhoeffer: 100 Reflections on the Christian Life*
(Abingdon, 2018)

*The Sanctuary for Lent 2017: Devotions with the
Protestant Reformers* (Abingdon, 2016)

# Daily Devotions *with* Herman Bavinck

## Believing and Growing in Christian Faith

### DONALD K. McKIM

P U B L I S H I N G
P.O. BOX 817 • PHILLIPSBURG • NEW JERSEY 08865-0817

Unless otherwise indicated, Scripture quotations are taken from the New Revised Standard Version Updated Edition. Copyright © 2021 National Council of Churches of Christ in the United States of America. Used by permission. All rights reserved worldwide.

Scripture quotations marked (KJV) are taken from the King James Version of the Bible.

Italics within Scripture quotations indicate emphasis added.

Cover art: Rembrandt van Rijn, *The Mill*, 1645/1648, oil on canvas, 34 1/2 x 41 9/16" (87.6 x 105.6 cm), Widener Collection, Courtesy of the National Gallery of Art, Washington, DC, https://www.nga.gov/collection/art-object-page.1201.html.

ISBN: 978-1-62995-781-4 (pbk)
ISBN: 978-1-62995-784-5 (ePub)

Printed in the United States of America

Library of Congress cataloging-in-publication data has been applied for.

Dedicated to the memory of

Gerrit Cornelis Berkouwer (1903–96)
Jack B. Rogers (1934–2016)

in thanksgiving to God for the lives, scholarship, and
witnesses of these two disciples of Jesus Christ (John 15:15)

# Contents

## Part 2: Living as a Christian

# Preface

I FIRST GOT acquainted with the Dutch Reformed theologian Herman Bavinck (1854–1921) in my days as a student at Westminster College (Pennsylvania).

Throughout my theological studies, Bavinck's understandings of Christian faith have been helpful to me. Bavinck was primarily a dogmatician, one who explains the meanings of Christian theology and Christian faith. But I have also found that his emphases are nourishing for the living of Christian life, as they flow from deep and rich theological understandings.

Christian faith and Christian life coalesce in *Daily Devotions with Herman Bavinck: Believing and Growing in Christian Faith*. This is one of a number of books I have written in the past decade that are "theologically devotional" in nature. In these, I try to acquaint readers with the thoughts of major theologians by providing a discussion of a few sentences from their writings. I hope to explain what the theologian meant and combine this with comments about the importance of these thoughts for our Christian living today. I hope in this way to provide accessible devotional readings that can nourish the minds and the hearts of those who read them.

From the writings of Herman Bavinck, I have selected quotations that can instruct and—I hope—inspire us to deepen our knowledge of Christian faith as well as our commitment and devotion to living out the implications of what we believe. Doctrine and life went together for Bavinck. He was a stalwart proponent of the Reformed faith rooted in the Protestant

Reformation and expressed in sixteenth-century Reformers such as John Calvin and Heinrich Bullinger as well as their theological successors. For Bavinck, the Reformed faith is a living faith—a faith that expresses itself in the everyday lives of Christian people. I hope that as we read Bavinck's words our Christian knowledge and experience can grow in vitality for us.

This book is dedicated to the memories of my beloved teacher and friend, Jack B. Rogers (1934–2016), and the Dutch theologian Gerrit Cornelis (G. C.) Berkouwer (1903–96). I am deeply grateful for their ministries of scholarship in the Reformed tradition and for their emphases on Christian living in the church in obedience to Jesus Christ.

Great thanks are due to my friends at P&R Publishing. Bryce Craig, Dave Almack, Amanda Martin, and Kim McKeever are superb publishing professionals as well as fine people. Their interest, support, and advice have been invaluable throughout this project. I am most grateful to them for their many kindnesses.

My life and work are enriched beyond measure by my family. My dear wife, LindaJo, loves and blesses me in our daily lives to bring the greatest joys. I thank you, LindaJo, as ever. Our sons and their families bring us wonder upon wonder. We are blessed by Stephen and Caroline and our grandchildren: Maddie, Annie, Jack, and Ford; and Karl and Lauren. We could not be more grateful for the gift of family love that we share together. We thank God!

Donald K. McKim
Germantown, Tennessee

# Introduction

HERMAN BAVINCK (December 13, 1854–July 29, 1921) was one of the most significant Reformed theologians of the nineteenth century. Along with Abraham Kuyper (1837–1920), Bavinck helped to revive and reinvigorate Reformed theology in the Netherlands. Through his writings, Bavinck affected Reformed thought in wide areas. His works are still read with appreciation and valued today. Theologically, Bavinck was compatible in many ways with the major American Reformed Presbyterian theologians of Princeton Theological Seminary: Charles Hodge (1797–1878) and Benjamin B. Warfield (1851–1921).

Bavinck's father, Jan Bavinck, was a minister in the Dutch Reformed Secessed Church. Herman Bavinck studied theology at Leiden and wrote his doctoral dissertation on *The Ethics of Ulrich Zwingli* (1880). He became a professor at the Theological Seminary of the Secessed Church at Kampen (1883) until he was called to become professor of systematic theology at the Free University of Amsterdam (1902).

While at Kampen, Bavinck published a four-volume work on dogmatics (theology) titled *Gereformeerd Dogmatiek* (1895–1901). Bavinck showed the value of the old Reformed theology in the context of contemporary, modern times. God is the object of theology. Holy Scripture is the source of our knowledge of God, made known by the work of the Holy Spirit to bring faith. Faith leads to understanding. The task of theology is to understand the knowledge of God. We appropriate this knowledge of God through faith in Jesus Christ. G. C. Berkouwer said Bavinck was "sensitive to the dangers of dead orthodoxy, of a confession that one believed in place of a living faith that one confessed."[1]

Bavinck visited the United States to give lectures at Princeton Theological Seminary on Calvinism (1898) and the philosophy of revelation (1908). Bavinck and Warfield agreed on the major dimensions of Reformed theology, though they had some differences, particularly on apologetics and Bavinck's book *The Certainty of Faith*. But in reviewing that book, Warfield wrote of his Dutch counterpart, "We must not close without emphasizing the delight we take in Dr. Bavinck's writings. In them extensive learning, sound thinking and profound religious feeling are smelted intimately together into a product of singular charm."[2]

In recent years, interest in Bavinck's work has accelerated. Portions of Bavinck's works were published in English through the efforts of the Dutch Reformed Translation Society, based in Grand Rapids, Michigan; and through the editorship of John Bolt and the translations of John Vriend, four volumes of Bavinck's *Reformed Dogmatics* have been published (2003–8). These were followed by an abridged one-volume edition (2011) and two of a proposed three volumes of Bavinck's *Reformed Ethics* (2019; 2021).

Additionally, a number of books on aspects of Bavinck's theology have appeared by authors such as Cory C. Brock, Bruce R. Pass, and Nathaniel Gray Sutanto, to name just a few.[3]

1. G. C. Berkouwer, *A Half Century of Theology*, ed. and trans. Lewis B. Smedes (Grand Rapids: Eerdmans, 1977), 14.

2. B. B. Warfield in *The Princeton Theological Review* 1 (1903): 148. See pages 138–48 for Warfield's review of Herman Bavinck, *De Zekerheid des Geloofs* (Kampen, Netherlands: Kok, 1901), translated as *The Certainty of Faith* by Harry der Nederlanden (St. Catherines, ON: Paideia Press, 1980).

3. See Cory C. Brock, *Orthodox Yet Modern: Herman Bavinck's Use of Friedrich Schleiermacher* (Bellingham, WA: Lexham Press, 2020); Bruce R. Pass, *The Heart of Dogmatics: Christology and Christocentrism in Herman Bavinck* (Göttingen, Germany: Vandenhock & Ruprecht, 2020); and Nathaniel Gray Sutanto, *God and Knowledge: Herman Bavinck's Theological Epistemology* (New York: T&T Clark, 2020).

James Eglinton's *Bavinck: A Critical Biography* (2020) is superb, giving us an unsurpassed resource.[4] Eglinton has also written a piece to introduce Bavinck to a wider audience: "Everybody Loves Bavinck: How a Dutch Neo-Calvinist Thinker Became the Latest Christian Theologian-Du-Jour."[5]

James Eglinton reminds us of some words of Bavinck as he was dying, which sum up what for Bavinck was most important in this life . . . and in death. Bavinck said, "My dogmatics avails me nothing, nor my knowledge, but I have my faith and in this I have all."[6] *In faith I have all.*

May this book deepen our Christian understandings and our Christian faith!

4. James Eglinton, *Bavinck: A Critical Biography* (Grand Rapids: Baker Academic Books), 2020.

5. James Eglinton, "Everybody Loves Bavinck: How a Dutch Neo-Calvinist Thinker Became the Latest Christian Theologian-Du-Jour," *Christianity Today*, February 18, 2022, https://www.christianitytoday.com/ct/2022/february-web -only/herman-bavinck-dutch-calvinist-theologian.html.

6.James Eglinton, *Trinity and Organism: Towards a New Reading of Herman Bavinck's Organic Motif* (London: Bloomsbury T&T Clark, 2012), 28.

# Using This Book

THIS BOOK PROVIDES reflections on quotations from the nineteenth-century Dutch Reformed theologian Herman Bavinck (1854–1921). The reflections convey the theological meaning of what Bavinck wrote as well as give implications of what his words mean for Christians today.

The book is intended for both personal and group use. Church groups can use it as a basis for reflection and discussion. Individuals can reflect on the pieces as a devotional dimension of their Christian living. Each entry features a biblical passage or verse at the beginning and a prayer point or question for discussion at the end of the piece.

The book is divided into two parts: "Believing as a Christian" and "Living as a Christian." These are general categories into which the devotions fall. The pieces can be used in the order in which they appear or in any other order. To give a further flavor of Bavinck's writings, a number of excerpts from Bavinck's works have been included among the devotions.

Several suggestions may be helpful for using this book.

*Read the Scripture passage and the devotion.* Each piece is written compactly, so each sentence is important. You can think about the meaning of each sentence as you read it in a contemplative manner. After reading a sentence, you may pause and reflect on its meaning.

*Meditate on the quotation and the devotion.* Bavinck's quotation is found in the midst of the devotion. As you think and meditate on the devotion and Bavinck's words, you may ask:

- What is Bavinck saying here?
- What do Bavinck's thoughts mean for the life of the church?
- What do Bavinck's thoughts mean for my own beliefs and life of faith?
- What new attitudes am I being led to discover through Bavinck's comments?
- How can Bavinck's thought be put into practice in the life of the church community and in my own life?

*Pray about this devotion.* Use the prayer point or question for discussion to orient your prayers or your discussion of this piece with other people. Ask God's Holy Spirit to lead and guide you into ways God wants you to believe and to live.

*Act on the insights you receive.* Ask yourself directly, "In what ways are the teachings I've received here leading me to stronger, deeper, and more informed belief in Christian faith? How am I being led to stronger, more committed ways of Christian living?" Then follow new insights and directions according to God's will as the Holy Spirit leads you.

The title of each devotion is a phrase that may bring the devotion's key insights to mind. When you look through the titles of the devotions, recall the important meanings and understandings that emerged for you from each piece.

If you keep a personal journal, you may wish to summarize what the devotions, quotations, or reflections mean to you. Be specific in indicating ways your life can be affected. Periodically, you can review these summaries through the days ahead.

"Selected Resources for Further Reflection" and other resources are found at the end of the book. These can encourage you to pursue more of Herman Bavinck's works and works about Bavinck.

# PART 1

# BELIEVING AS A CHRISTIAN

# 1.

# Theology Leads to Adoration and Worship

*Father, the hour has come; glorify your Son so that the Son may glorify you, since you have given him authority over all people, to give eternal life to all whom you have given him. And this is eternal life, that they may know you, the only true God, and Jesus Christ, whom you have sent. (John 17:1–3)*

STUDYING THEOLOGY TAKES place in many ways. Some undertake formal theological studies in seminaries. In the church, Christian believers study their faith, focusing on Scripture and church doctrines (teachings). Reading theology, talking theology, or listening to theology can take place formally or informally in our daily lives.

What is the purpose of learning Christian theology? We can have many purposes, but Bavinck believed one stood out. Scripture is the source of theology—it is God's revelation of who God is and what God has done. The knowledge of God is "one central dogma" to which all theology points, said Bavinck. Theology always focuses on God and God alone. The more theology reflects on God, Bavinck believed, "the more it will be moved to adoration and worship."

This makes studying theology "superlatively fruitful for life." Can you think of anything more important than knowing God—and being led by that knowledge into the adoration and worship of God? Theology is not abstract talk—just "ideas" that are removed from real life. No! Theology is eminently practical—and livable—because it deals with our most basic need: to know who God is and what God has done.

Our knowledge of God, as God is revealed in Jesus Christ, is the fullness of life itself (Ps. 89:15; Isa. 11:9; Jer. 31:34). Jesus pointed to this when he said, "And this is eternal life, that they may know you, the only true God, and Jesus Christ, whom you have sent" (John 17:3). John Calvin pointed to this in the first question and answer of the 1545 Geneva Catechism: "What is the chief end of human life? To know God by whom [humans] were created." Our knowledge of God our Creator and Redeemer comes to us through Scripture and through the study of theology based on Scripture.

May our studies of theology—however they take place—lead us to a deeper knowledge of God and of Jesus Christ, whom God has sent. May we be led to deeper adoration and worship as we praise the living God!

**Prayer Point:** Spend time in prayer praising and thanking God for the ways you know who God is and what God does. Remember theological insights you have gained, and let them lead you to deeper prayers of adoration and the worship of God.

# 2.

# Faith in Christ and Scripture

*We also constantly give thanks to God for this,*
*that when you received the word of God that you*
*heard from us you accepted it not as a human*
*word but as what it really is, God's word, which is*
*also at work in you believers. (1 Thess. 2:13)*

W E KNOW OF Jesus Christ only through the Holy Scriptures. The Bible is the source of our knowledge of God—who God is and what God has done. Central to Scripture is God's love for the world, which is known to us most fully in God's sending Christ to live and die and be raised again for our salvation. This is the gospel message: "For God so loved the world that he gave his only Son, so that everyone who believes in him may not perish but may have eternal life" (John 3:16). In the Bible we find Christ offered to us by God—as John Calvin said, "clothed with his gospel."

As we hear and accept the message of Christ, we also hear and accept the Scriptures through whom Christ is presented to us. We receive Christ and the Scriptures by faith. Faith focuses on Jesus Christ as the object of our faith, and faith receives the Scriptures through whom Jesus Christ is known to us. As Bavinck put it, "Faith . . . reaches out in a single act to the person

23

of Christ as well as to Scripture. It embraces Christ as Savior and Scripture as the word of God." As Paul told the Thessalonians, he was thankful the people received the message of Christ "as what it really is, God's word" (1 Thess. 2:13).

Today, Scripture leads us to Christ and Christ comes to us in the Scriptures. We receive Christ and the Scriptures by faith. There is the closest possible relation between Scripture and Christ because Scripture is the way by which the person and message of Jesus Christ is made known to us. Martin Luther said the Scriptures are the cradle in which Christ lies. So we need to use every means possible to understand more fully the message of God's Word. So through this msg we meet X.

This is our great cause for thanks to God and gratitude. God gives us the means of knowing Jesus Christ as our Lord and Savior through Scripture as God's Word. The Scriptures are a means of God's grace. Let us rejoice in faith!

**Prayer Point:** Pray that in Jesus Christ, God's Word will be "a lamp to [your] feet and a light to [your] path" (Ps. 119:105).

# 3.

# The Spirit Bears Witness

*All who are led by the Spirit of God are children of
God. For you did not receive a spirit of slavery to fall
back into fear, but you received a spirit of adoption.
When we cry, "Abba! Father!" it is that very Spirit
bearing witness with our spirit that we are children
of God, and if children, then heirs: heirs of God
and joint heirs with Christ. (Rom. 8:14–17)*

T HE BIBLE MAY not mean anything special to someone for
many years. The Bible? Their attitude is "Take it or leave it."
But at some point, the Scriptures become supremely important
to them. The Scriptures, which were once like dead letters, now
become the words of a wonderful new way of life: life lived by
faith in Jesus Christ.

What makes the difference? Bavinck noted that "it is the
Spirit of God alone who can make a person inwardly certain of
the truth of divine revelation." God's Holy Spirit gives us faith
in Jesus Christ, and with that faith comes the assurance that
Scripture is the Word of God. No number of intellectual argu-
ments or logical deductions can bring the certainty of faith that
the Holy Spirit brings to our minds and hearts. Paul affirmed
that "it is that very Spirit bearing witness with our spirit that

we are children of God" (Rom. 8:16; see also 1 Cor. 12:3). The Spirit points us to Scripture to find God's reaching out in love to save us by sending Jesus Christ (Rom. 5:8).

The Holy Spirit has given us Scripture. The Spirit inspired biblical writers to convey God's Word in the written words of the Scriptures (2 Tim. 3:16; 2 Peter 1:21). God's Spirit also "bears witness"—or points us toward the Scriptures—so that in faith we recognize the Bible as God's Word, God speaking to us. The Bible "comes alive" for us now. In Scripture, we experience God's presence and power, supremely in Jesus Christ. The "external word"—the Bible—becomes the "internal word": God's Word speaking directly and personally to us. Our whole selves are bound to the Scriptures by the witness of God's Spirit. This is, as theologians say, the "testimony of the Holy Spirit."

We have the inner assurance that Scripture is the Word of God. We do not have to prove the Bible. The Spirit's witness gives us the deepest confidence that in Scripture, God is addressing us and, through our union with Christ, is at work within us!

**Prayer Point:** Pray for God's Holy Spirit to illuminate your mind and heart to hear God's Word to you in Scripture every day.

SC, JG, JG, BG, ✓
PC, PE, CF,

# 4.

# Certainty Flows from Faith

*I am not ashamed, for I know the one in whom I have*
*put my trust, and I am sure that he is able to guard the*
*deposit I have entrusted to him. Hold to the standard*
*of sound teaching that you have heard from me, in the*
*faith and love that are in Christ Jesus. (2 Tim. 1:12–13)*

ONE THING WE often crave in life is certainty. We want to
be sure of things. We want to know "for sure" that our
investments are secure . . . or even if it will rain tomorrow!
Certainty is important.

So also in faith. Christian faith brings our conviction that
God has acted in Jesus Christ to forgive our sin and give us
eternal life. This is a certainty at the very core of our beings
as Christian people. Bavinck said this faith is "a restoration of
the right relationship between God and man, the return of the
trust" a child places in its parent. "Certainty is included by its
very nature" in human expressions of faith—even more so in
faith that believes in Jesus Christ as God's Son, our Savior. In
faith, we believe the gospel promises of who Jesus is and what
he has done to bring salvation. Faith also brings the certainty
that by God's grace, "we too share in these promises."

This means, wrote Bavinck, that faith "does not attain certainty regarding itself through logical reasoning nor through constantly examining itself and reflecting on its own nature. . . . But certainty flows to us immediately and directly out of faith itself. Certainty is an essential characteristic of faith; it is inseparable from it and belongs to its nature."

What a blessed joy! Our certainty in faith is not generated by us—by our thinking or our efforts. Instead, faith flows from "the promises of God, the gospel, which poses no conditions but only proclaims that everything has been accomplished. . . . All we have to do," continued Bavinck, is "enter into that accomplished work and rest in it for eternity." We can affirm the Christian's confession: "I know the one in whom I have put my trust, and I am sure that he is able to guard the deposit I have entrusted to him" (2 Tim. 1:12). In faith, we have the certainty that God's promises in Jesus Christ are for us, now and forever.

**Prayer Point:** Pray often in praise and thanks to God for the gift of faith in Jesus Christ and for the certainty that you have in sharing all the gospel promises.

# 5.

# Center and Periphery
# of Scripture

*Sacred writings . . . are able to instruct you for
salvation through faith in Christ Jesus. All scripture
is inspired by God and is useful for teaching,
for reproof, for correction, and for training in
righteousness, so that the person of God may be . . .
equipped for every good work. (2 Tim. 3:15–17)*

THE REFORMED TRADITION, emerging during the sixteenth-century Reformation period, has stressed that each part of Scripture is to be read and understood in its relation to the overall message of salvation that the Bible presents.

Bavinck's way of expressing this was his concept of the "organic inspiration" of Scripture. He used the image of the human body to say there is a "center" and a "periphery" of Scripture. Bavinck wrote, "In the human organism nothing is accidental, neither its length, nor its breadth, nor its color or its tint. This is not however, to say that everything is equally connected with its life center. The head and the heart occupy a much more important place in the body than the hand and the foot, and these again are greatly superior in value to the nails and the hair."

For Bavinck, this did not imply differences in the inspiration of Scripture itself, or various grades of inspiration. All Scripture is inspired (2 Tim. 3:16). Scripture includes both divine and human dimensions. Bavinck wrote that Scripture is "totally human in all its parts but also divine in all its parts." But each part of Scripture has its own function to carry out. Some parts are more centrally important for Scripture than others. For instance, John 3:16 is closer to Scripture's central message than Psalm 120:4: "A warrior's sharp arrows, with glowing coals of the broom tree!" Both verses are inspired by God and are part of the Bible. But they function in different ways. Compared to other verses, John 3:16—which has been called "the gospel in a nutshell"—is more clearly and closely related to Scripture's overall story of salvation and its message of who God is and what God has done, what Bavinck called the message of "the saving knowledge of God."

Scripture is authoritative because it is inspired by God. For Bavinck, "Scripture is the word of God because the Holy Spirit testifies in it concerning Christ, because it has the Word-made-flesh as its matter and content."

Scripture is God's divine revelation, inspired by God and given to us for our salvation.

**Reflection Point:** Consider the importance of recognizing that the Bible is both a "divine" and a "human" book that works to convey God's revelation.

# Special Revelation

*The sigh rises from the depths of man's heart: "If only God would tear the heavens asunder and come down to earth. . . ." We always see man at work, whether, by acquiring knowledge, by keeping all kinds of commandments, or by withdrawing from the world into the secrecy of his own mind, he can partake of redemption from evil and fellowship with God; here all man's work falls away, and it is God himself who acts, intervenes in history, paves the way of redemption in Christ, and by the power of his grace leads man therein and makes him walk. The special revelation is the answer that God himself gives in word and deed to the questions that arise in the human heart through his own guidance.*

# 6.

# The Heart and Core
# of Our Confession

*Go therefore and make disciples of all nations,*
*baptizing them in the name of the Father and of*
*the Son and of the Holy Spirit. (Matt. 28:19)*

B ASIC TO CHRISTIAN faith is our belief in God as the divine Trinity. We confess one God who is Father, Son, and Holy Spirit. We believe in one God in three persons. The Trinity is three distinct persons in the one divine being.

This belief emerged in the early Christian centuries. On the basis of the Old and New Testaments and consideration of the overall witness of the Scriptures, the church affirmed its faith in the triune God: God as three persons in unity. In the familiar Apostles' Creed, we confess that we believe in God the Father, Jesus Christ, and the Holy Spirit as the three persons of the one God. The Trinity revealed to us is identical with the Trinity that is the very nature of God. We trust this God; we surrender ourselves to this God. This is the God of our life and our salvation. The church baptizes Christians in the triune name (Matt. 28:16–20).

Bavinck maintained that "the Article of Faith of the Holy Trinity is the heart and core of our confession, the distinguishing mark of the Christian religion, the [praise] and the consolation of all true Christ-believers." The doctrine of the Trinity is not abstract theological speculation. The Holy Trinity is the living God who is to be worshiped, adored, and served. The triune God is with us throughout our lives—in all situations—saving us, helping us, and bringing us comfort and hope. The three persons of the Trinity can be known; their work in the world, the church, and our lives can be recognized. God's presence with us—as Father, Son, and Holy Spirit—is the deepest reality we know, in life and in death.

"Thus," wrote Bavinck, "the confession of the Trinity is the core and the main element of the entire Christian religion. Without it, neither creation, nor redemption, nor sanctification can be purely maintained." We cannot explain everything about the Trinity. But we can worship the triune God who is revealed as our Creator, Redeemer, and Sustainer. We praise "God in three persons, blessed Trinity"!

**Reflection Point:** Think of the three persons of the Trinity and what Scripture says about each of them. Contemplate the ways you are aware of the work of the Trinity in the world, the church, and your own life.

# The Divine Trinity

*The church confesses ... [that] God is above the world, distinct from it in essence, and yet with his whole being in it at the present time and nowhere, in no point of space and for no moment of time separated from it. He is both distant and near—highly exalted and at the same time deeply ingrained in all his creatures. He is our Creator, who, distinct from his being, brought us forth by his will. He is our Redeemer, who saves us, not by our works but by the riches of his grace. He is our Sanctifier, who dwells in us as in his temple. As a triune God, he is a God above and for and in us.*

# 7.

# The Fountain of All Good

*They feast on the abundance of your house,*
*and you give them drink from the river of your delights.*
*For with you is the fountain of life;*
*in your light we see light.*
*O continue your steadfast love to those who know you*
*and your salvation to the upright of heart! (Ps. 36:8–10)*

WE ADMIRE CERTAIN characteristics and even virtues in people we meet. We are glad when we encounter wisdom in a wise person, or goodness in a person with a good heart, or justice in an upright person, or mercy in a person who extends compassion. We are thankful for people who live in such ways.

But how do we recognize these characteristics, and why do we admire them? From whence do they spring in people's lives?

Bavinck spoke of God as "the abundant fountain of all good." All the good we experience in life has its origin in God. God is the supreme good, and from God flows all the good we know and encounter. God is the fountain. We remember the psalmist wrote, "For with you is the fountain of life; in your light we see light" (Ps. 36:9). God is the fountain of life—and God is the "fountain of all good."

Bavinck explained this theologically. He wrote that God's "attributes coincide with his being. Every quality is his essence." By this he meant that God is "not only wise and true, good and holy, just and merciful"—those virtues we admire. But God *is* "wisdom, truth, goodness, holiness, justice and mercy themselves." God acts in these ways (God's attributes) because these ways express who God is (God's being). God is "therefore also the origin and fountainhead of all those virtues which are present in creatures." All these virtues originate in God. God is "all that he has and the source of all that creatures have." All we have—any wisdom, goodness, justice, mercy—comes from God who *is* all those things in God's own self. God's "attributes coincide with his being," said Bavinck. For God is "the abundant fountain of all good."

This means for us that all the characteristics or virtues we admire are grounded in God's own self. God acts in these ways—because this is who God is. And God communicates these elements of goodness . . . to us. All praise to God, "the abundant fountain of all good"!

**Reflection Point:** Reflect thankfully on persons you know who show characteristics that emerge from God as the "fountain of all good." Reflect on ways these characteristics—which point to God—are present in your own life.

# 8.

# God's Covenant of Grace

*Just as I swore that the waters of Noah*
*would never again go over the earth,*
*so I have sworn that I will not be angry with you*
*and will not rebuke you.*
*For the mountains may depart*
*and the hills be removed,*
*but my steadfast love shall not depart from you,*
*and my covenant of peace shall not be removed,*
*says the LORD, who has compassion on you.*
*(Isa. 54:9–10)*

THERE ARE MANY ways to ask what is the big picture of the Bible. What is the main thing the Bible says? What does the Bible most want us to know?

One appropriate answer would be that the Bible wants to tell us about the covenant of grace.

The covenant of grace is God's purpose to save sinful people. Bavinck said, "God taught his people in the first place that the covenant of grace, with all its goods and benefits, was due solely to his mercy; it had its origin and basis in his undeserved mercy: 'I will be gracious to whom I will be gracious and will show mercy on whom I will show mercy' (Exod. [33:19])." After humanity's fall into sin (Gen. 3), God was at work in different ways, using leaders and prophets through the history of Israel. Finally God in Jesus Christ brought salvation and reconciliation, granting us "eternal life by grace through faith in Christ," said Bavinck.

In the Old and New Testaments, "the covenant of grace is one." Those who believe God's promise have "the same trust in the grace of God that opens the access to salvation then and now. And the same benefits of forgiveness and regeneration, of renewal and eternal life, were then and are now given to the faithful. They all walk on the same path, even though the light differs in brightness, which [illuminates] the faithful of the Old and New Testaments."

The "one great, all-encompassing promise of the covenant of grace is this: 'I will be your God and the God of your seed'" (Ex. 6:7; Lev. 26:12). This promise is grounded in God and depends on God, who is unchangeable and faithful: "People may become unfaithful, but God does not forget his promise. He cannot and must not break his covenant." God pardons sins (Isa. 43:25; Jer. 14:21) and will not falter (Isa. 54:10).

Now God's covenant of grace is fulfilled in Jesus Christ, through the "new covenant in [his] blood" (Luke 22:20). In Christ, God's merciful purpose to save sinners is proclaimed and God's promise of grace continues—for us!

**Reflection Point:** Reflect on the history of salvation throughout the Bible. Think of how God's mercy is extended, how sin could be forgiven, and how examples of believing and trusting God's promise are found throughout different biblical periods. Think then of how salvation comes to us now in Jesus Christ.

# 9.

# God Alone Saves

*While we were still weak, at the right time Christ
died for the ungodly. . . . If while we were enemies
we were reconciled to God through the death of his
Son, much more surely, having been reconciled,
will we be saved by his life. (Rom. 5:6, 10)*

THERE IS A message about our faith we need to hear over
and over again.

We need to hear this message because it is easy for our
faith to slip away from it. We may easily lose sight of this basic
conviction that is key to Christian faith and particularly to the
Reformed theological tradition.

The message is *God alone saves!*

Bavinck pointed out that "all other religions try to obtain
salvation by the works of men, but Christianity makes a strong
protest against this. . . . It does not preach self-redemption,
but glories in redemption by Christ alone." Our faith is not
"do it yourself," or "lift yourself up by your own bootstraps,"
or a system in which persons have to achieve certain things
or perform certain actions to ensure their salvation or right
relationship with God. No. Those are "self-help" approaches
that are directly opposite to the Christian gospel.

41

Our Christian faith, and especially the Reformed faith, stresses that humans do not save themselves and do not "save God, but God alone saves" us—the whole person—"for eternity," as Bavinck wrote. God alone saves through God's actions, not by what humans do. Our redemption is in "Christ alone"—in Jesus Christ whom God sent to save us (John 3:16), who died and was raised again for our justification (salvation) (Rom. 4:25). Our salvation is in Christ, through whom God reached out to human sinners to forgive and reconcile us who are estranged from God (Rom. 5:10; Col. 1:21).

God alone saves, through Jesus Christ. So Christianity, as Bavinck says, "is a religion not of works, but of faith; not of merits, but of grace." Salvation is by grace alone, through faith alone, and by the work of God alone—none of this being of human origin or our own making.

This is why the Christian gospel is literally "good news"! Our eternal salvation does not rest on human efforts or achievements. Salvation is God's gracious gift—he gives us the faith to believe that Jesus Christ died for our sins and has brought us new life by the Holy Spirit.

We give all glory to God!

**Reflection Point:** Think of how great a difference there is between the Christian faith and "religious systems" that teach that the way to ultimate fulfillment or blessedness is achieved by human actions.

# 10.

# The Counsel of God

*With all wisdom and insight he has made known to us*
*the mystery of his will, according to his good pleasure*
*that he set forth in Christ, as a plan for the fullness of*
*time, to gather up all things in him. . . . In Christ we*
*have also obtained an inheritance, having been destined*
*according to the purpose of him who accomplishes all*
*things according to his counsel and will. (Eph. 1:8–11)*

B AVINCK AND THE Reformed theological tradition emphasized that "God brings about everything according to his counsel." God's counsel is the divine will: God's eternal plan and purposes for all things that come to pass.

All God's works emerge from God's counsel, from the creation of the world onward. We see through emphases in Scripture—such as the creation of humanity—that this creation was an expression of God's will to create. Also, God wanted to create humans in the "image" and "likeness" of God (Gen. 1:26). This gives us a unique relationship with our Creator.

So also in redemption. As Paul wrote, "In Christ we have also obtained an inheritance, having been destined according to the purpose of him who accomplishes all things according to his counsel and will" (Eph. 1:11; see also Rom. 8:29). By God's grace and mercy (Eph. 2:8), God chooses to save people (Eph. 1:4) by giving them the gift of faith in Jesus Christ. Christ is the Mediator between God and humanity. Through his death, human sin is forgiven and new life is given to those reconciled with God (2 Cor. 5:17–21). Bavinck wrote that "God's intention is nothing less than to appoint Christ the Mediator as the head of the congregation and to form the congregation into the body of Christ (1 Cor. 12:12, 27; Eph. 1:22, 23; 4:16)." God creates new persons in Christ by the work of the Holy Spirit in regeneration (John 3:3), faith (1 Cor. 12:3), adoption (Rom. 8:15), renewal (Titus 3:5), and sealing until the day of redemption (Eph. 1:13; 4:30).

This led Bavinck to write that "the love of the Father, the grace of the Son, and the fellowship of the Holy Spirit are fixed for the people of the Lord in the eternal and unchangeable counsel of God." The counsel of God shows us that "salvation is God's work from beginning to end, the divine work par excellence."

The counsel of God, said Bavinck, is "therefore also unspeakably rich in consolation." For "no blind chance, no dark fate" governs the world. But "all . . . rests in the hands of an all-powerful God and a merciful Father."

**Prayer Point:** Give thanks that God's counsel is the supreme power in the universe and that God's counsel can be trusted. Be grateful for the comfort of believing and relying on our benevolent God in all things.

# 11.

# Election

*Blessed be the God and Father of our Lord Jesus Christ, who has blessed us in Christ with every spiritual blessing in the heavenly places, just as he chose us in Christ before the foundation of the world to be holy and blameless before him in love. He destined us for adoption as his children through Jesus Christ, according to the good pleasure of his will. (Eph. 1:3–5)*

A PART OF the good news of the Christian gospel is that our salvation in Jesus Christ does not rest on us, on what we do for God. Our salvation, through and through, rests on what God does for us. God sent Jesus Christ to be our Savior. God gives the gift of the Holy Spirit to bring us a new relationship with God through faith. God chooses or elects us to have faith and receive the gift of salvation. Salvation is God's work in us!

Election is "God's gracious intention," Bavinck wrote, "according to which he has predestined those whom he has known in love to be conformed to the image of his Son (Rom. 8:29). Election is not grounded in those persons, but only in God's grace; the Lord has mercy on whom he has mercy, and he is merciful toward whom he is merciful" (see Rom. 9:15–16). God's grace is electing grace, initiating salvation. Bavinck continued, "Faith is a gift of God (Eph. 2:8); the faithful were chosen in Christ before the foundation of the world that in time they might come to faith and through that faith be holy and blameless before God (Eph. 1:4)."

The focus of faith, which is the gift of God given to us by the Holy Spirit (John 3:3–8), is Jesus Christ. God's election is the cause of the faith that we have been given and that we know as a reality in our lives. So election is not a speculative doctrine—"Am I elected?" Election is the good news that our salvation is a gift of God. We are saved by God's grace alone—received by us through faith by the work of the Holy Spirit. Since our faith is directed toward Christ our Savior, the only question we need to ask about election is "Do I believe in Jesus Christ?" If you do, it means God has given the gift of faith, by God's grace—and thus you have been chosen by God's gracious election. We are saved by the will of God, by God's "good pleasure." In gratitude and praise . . . we rejoice.

**Reflection Point:** Think of how important it is for you to realize that your salvation and the faith through which salvation comes are gifts of God and not of your own doing. List various ways this is a blessing for you.

# 12.

# Christian Faith Is Pure Grace

*God, who is rich in mercy, out of the great love with*
*which he loved us even when we were dead through*
*our trespasses, made us alive together with Christ—*
*by grace you have been saved—and raised us up*
*with him and seated us with him in the heavenly*
*places in Christ Jesus, so that in the ages to come he*
*might show the immeasurable riches of his grace in*
*kindness toward us in Christ Jesus. (Eph. 2:4–7)*

W E ARE MOST accustomed to gaining things by our own
efforts. This is a lesson we learn early. We have to work or
strive or try to get what we desire since we cannot depend on its
coming to us in any other way. The phrase *working lives* describes
what we do: work to make a living—or even to make a life.

In Christian faith, however, what is most important—our
relationship with God—is not something we can work to
achieve by ourselves. Our salvation restores the relationship
of trust and love that God desires to have with sinful people.
Because we are sinful, we cannot establish this relationship with
God by ourselves.

But, says Bavinck, though as humans we have "forfeited" our
salvation and can "never again acquire" it by our "own efforts,"

God does not abandon us. "Freely and by grace," God grants salvation. But, importantly, this salvation does not depend on human "works" in which we must "first fulfill some condition in order to share eternal life." This would turn salvation into some human achievement. Instead of works, we are saved by God's grace—the gift of God—in Jesus Christ.

Thus, wrote Bavinck, "grace and works are here opposed to each other and mutually exclusive. If it is by grace, it is no longer of works, otherwise grace is no longer grace. And if it is by works, then it is no longer grace, otherwise the work is no longer work." Our natural inclination to work for what we can achieve is not the way we receive salvation from God!

This is what we find:

> By grace you have been saved through faith, and this is not your own doing; it is the gift of God—not the result of works, so that no one may boast. (Eph. 2:8–9)

Salvation is God's free gift, which God gives to us in Jesus Christ. So Bavinck wrote that "the Christian religion has the peculiar characteristic of being the religion of salvation, pure grace, pure religion." Christian faith—pure grace!

**Prayer Point:** Pray in praise to God for the sheer grace of God in providing salvation in Christ as a free gift. Thank God for the gift of faith and ask God to help you to proclaim God's free grace to others.

# 13.

# The Purpose of All World History

*Do not worry, saying, "What will we eat?" or "What will we drink?" or "What will we wear?" For it is the gentiles who seek all these things, and indeed your heavenly Father knows that you need all these things. But seek first the kingdom of God and his righteousness, and all these things will be given to you as well. (Matt. 6:31–33)*

SOMETIMES, IF WE reflect for a few minutes, we may ask ourselves, What is the great purpose of history? What is the big story of human existence? Why do humans live? What is our highest good?

Bavinck wrote an essay called "The Kingdom of God, the Highest Good." In this piece, he asserted that the "kingdom of God is the essential content, the core, and the purpose of all of world history." This is a big claim! But it does give us a vision that can orient our lives and give us purpose for all our days.

Jesus pointed us to this comprehensive vision for the life of the world and our own lives. Jesus spoke more about the "kingdom of God" than he did about any other subject. He put it clearly to his disciples: "But seek first the kingdom of God and his righteousness, and all these things will be given to you as well" (Matt. 6:33). Jesus spoke of the human desire to gain "treasure" and "wealth" (6:19–24) and to "worry" about all manner of things that may trouble us (6:25–32). But through it all, we are to "seek first the kingdom of God."

God's kingdom is to come in all its fullness in the future. It will be marked by the complete rule and glorification of God— scenes like the ones we find in the book of Revelation (11:15–18). But "on our way to the kingdom" in its ultimate form, we live and seek God's kingdom here and now. We want to live according to the will of God, according to God's purposes, for the world and for our lives. This is our "core" reason for living as God's people, as disciples of Jesus Christ. God is carrying out God's divine purposes in history. As people of faith who are part of God's church, we can participate in God's kingdom activities. In our individual lives and in the broader sweep of all who have ever lived, God's kingdom is being established and is the ultimate "purpose of all of world history."

We can find our purpose for living as we follow in the way of Jesus and recognize the kingdom of God as our highest good— and the highest good for all the world!

**Reflection Question:** In what ways are you daily seeking God's kingdom and consciously trying to live out God's kingdom as Jesus showed us?

# 14.

# Christ Is the Turning Point of Time

*We were enslaved to the elemental principles of the*
*world. But when the fullness of time had come, God*
*sent his Son, born of a woman, born under the law, in*
*order to redeem those who were under the law, so that*
*we might receive adoption as children. (Gal. 4:3–5)*

WE ARE WELL familiar with the distinction between *before Christ* (BC) and *anno Domini* (AD), "the Year of our Lord."[1] These mark dates in relation to the birth of Jesus Christ. We do not know for certain what year Jesus was born (most locate his birth between 6 BC and 4 BC). But the traditional dating procedures distinguish between history "before Jesus's birth" and history that has occurred since Jesus was born. Jesus Christ impacts our calendars and all human history.

Theologically, the Old Testament describes time before the coming of Jesus, and the New Testament begins with the birth of Jesus. The Old Testament is the period of God's revelation of

---

1. An equivalent way of marking years is "Before the Common Era" (BCE) and "Common Era" (CE). But these too are determined by the birth of Jesus Christ.

"promise," and the New Testament is the period of God's revelation of "fulfillment" (Rom. 1:2). God promised the people of Israel a redeemer, a Messiah—a "coming one." For Christians, Jesus Christ is God's Messiah. Paul wrote,

> When the fullness of time had come, God sent his Son, born of a woman, born under the law, in order to redeem those who were under the law, so that we might receive adoption as children. (Gal. 4:4–5)

Jesus Christ is the revelation of God as a human being, the one who came to provide salvation and to reconcile sinful humans to God. The coming of Jesus Christ has permanently changed the world. Bavinck wrote that "whereas in the Old Testament everything was prepared for Christ, now everything is derived from him. Christ is the turning point of time."

Chronologically, BC and AD are two eras of history. But theologically, for all the world, Jesus Christ is the turning point of time. God's relationship to the world is now forever focused on Jesus Christ. Humanity's relationship to God is made new in the death and resurrection of Jesus Christ, in whom all the promises of God find their fulfillment (2 Cor. 1:20).

Jesus Christ is the turning point of our personal time. Our true lives are derived from Christ as we live in faith and union with him.

**Reflection Questions:** Perhaps you can remember when you expressed your faith in Jesus Christ as Lord and Savior. What differences do you see in your life before and after your confession of faith? In what ways did Jesus become the "turning point" for you?

# 15.

# The Wonderful Works of God

*At this sound the crowd gathered and was bewildered,*
*because each one heard them speaking in the native*
*language of each. . . . "In our own languages we hear*
*them speaking about God's deeds of power." (Acts 2:6, 11)*

T HE DAY OF Pentecost was a day of great importance for the
Christian church. The Holy Spirit descended on the apostles
of Jesus, who "were filled with the Holy Spirit and began to speak
in other languages, as the Spirit gave them ability" (Acts 2:4).
From then on, the Spirit was with the church, leading and guiding
women and men of faith who began to follow in the way of Jesus.

The record in Acts 2 is that the persons gathered that day
were "from every people under heaven living in Jerusalem" (2:5).
By the power of the Spirit "each one heard them [the apostles]
speaking" in their native language (2:6). These people were
"amazed and astonished," since the apostles were all "Galileans."

What was going on here? God's wonderful works were taking
place by the work of God the Holy Spirit. The people said, "In
our own languages we hear them speaking about God's deeds of
power" (2:11). The preaching of the "wonderful works of God"
began the spread of the Christian gospel of God's redeeming
love in Jesus Christ, known to us through the Holy Scriptures.

Bavinck described it this way:

> The Christian religion does not exist merely in words, in a doctrine, but that it is, in word and fact, a work of God, which was brought about in the past, is being worked out in the present, and will only be completed in the future. The content of the Christian faith is not a scientific theory, nor a philosophical formula for explaining the world, but a recognition and confession of the great works of God, which are being created through the ages, encompass the entire world, and will only be completed in the new heaven and the new earth, wherein dwells righteousness.

As Christians, we recognize and confess the great and wonderful works of God through all ages and throughout the whole world. Now and forever, we praise God's works that were made known at Pentecost and continue today in our lives.

**Prayer Point:** Pray in great thanks and joy for the wonderful works of God, especially those in your own life that you treasure in your heart.

# 16.

# Creation Rests
# on God's Good Pleasure

*You are worthy, our Lord and God,*
*to receive glory and honor and power,*
*for you created all things,*
*and by your will they existed and were created.*
*(Rev. 4:11)*

T HERE ARE MANY theories about creation. Scientific theories through the centuries seek to explain the origin of
creation—the earth and the cosmos.

These theories seek to explain *how* the world was created.
Theologians—on the basis of Holy Scripture—attempt to
explain *why* the world was created.

Theologically, the origin of the cosmos rests with God. God
is the source of all creation. Bavinck wrote, "Creation is entirely
a free act of God." Genesis 1:1 (KJV) says, "In the beginning
God created the heaven and the earth." The book of Revelation
conveys the praise of God for creating all things: "You are worthy,
our Lord and God, to receive glory and honor and power, for
you created all things, and by your will they existed and were
created" (Rev. 4:11).

Bavinck highlighted God's freedom in creation: "The creation rests solely on God's power, on his eternal good pleasure, on his absolute sovereignty." God's power enabled all things to be established. That there is a creation at all rests on God's choosing to create. Creation is an expression of God's "eternal good pleasure." God desired to create. God is sovereign over all things—absolutely so. No other rival power or alternative source of creative energy or force could do what God has done. God's "absolute sovereignty" means all things exist by God's power and from God's will and good pleasure in creating all things. Saints sing, "You created all things, and by your will they existed and were created" (Rev. 4:11). God's creative word ("God said . . .") is the source of all. God's sovereign will enables creation to occur.

The rest of the Bible describes God's relationship with creation—and with us, created humans. God's verdict on creation is "Indeed, it was very good" (Gen. 1:31). God's purposes in creating—the "why"—emerge as we read the story of salvation in Scripture. Our human purpose is to give God all praise and glory for being God the Creator.

**Prayer Point:** Contemplate God's creation and, in as many ways as you can, give God praise and thanks for God's "good pleasure" in creating all things.

# 17.

# God Maintains Creation

*Let all the earth fear the LORD;*
*let all the inhabitants of the world stand in awe of him,*
*for he spoke, and it came to be;*
*he commanded, and it stood firm. (Ps. 33:8–9)*

GOD IS CREATOR. God created all things. But God's work was not finished!

The continuing existence of creation—from our world to the whole cosmos—is the ongoing work of God. Bavinck wrote that "from God emanates power, almighty and divine power, as much for the continuation of the world as for its creation in the beginning. Without such power no creature could exist for a moment; in the same instant in which God withdrew his hand and withheld his power, it would sink into nothingness."

We take the world for granted, just as we often take our lives for granted. Things exist around us—they always have and, we think, they always will. But behind it all, behind all things "seen and unseen," is the sustaining, maintaining power of God. As hymnwriter Henry Hallam Tweedy put it,

Eternal God, whose power upholds
Both flower and flaming star.

Without this power, no creature would exist, and without God's power, the whole cosmos would "sink into nothingness," as Bavinck said. This ongoing maintenance or preservation of the world is part of God's providence. By providence, God provides "all that is necessary for the world" and "sustains the world from moment to moment."

When we praise and thank God for creating all things—including us—we should also remember to praise and thank God for continuing to preserve and maintain creation. The power that permits the ongoing existence of all things is God's power. This should make every moment of our existence special to us. All our moments are a gift from our Creator and Sustainer! God's Word and Spirit are the means by which all creation is upheld. The psalmist proclaimed of God, "He spoke, and it came to be; he commanded, and it stood firm" (Ps. 33:9). God does not let go. God creates and sustains, enabling us to live our lives in obedience to the One who created us and maintains our lives in all times.

**Prayer Point:** As you reflect on your life, pray in deep thanksgiving and praise for the ongoing power of God to maintain creation—and your own existence. Praise God for giving you each second of life.

# 18.

# Faith in God's Providence

*Whatever was written in former days was written*
*for our instruction, so that by steadfastness*
*and by the encouragement of the scriptures*
*we might have hope. (Rom. 15:4)*

THE WORLD AROUND us confronts us with much we cannot understand over the course of our lives. Much is unfathomable to us. We can feel confused and discouraged.

But we believe in God's providence. We believe God is at work in this world, preserving the world, working with humans to carry out God's purposes, and ultimately governing the world toward God's final, ultimate purposes in the eternal reign of God: "Hallelujah! For the Lord God the Almighty reigns" (Rev. 19:6)!

Our firm belief in God's providential purposes does not clear up all our questions about life. We know well what Bavinck meant when he wrote that "plenty of riddles remain, both in the life of individuals and in the history of the world and humankind."

But Bavinck continued to say that "God lets the light of his Word shine over all these enigmas and mysteries, not to solve them, but that 'by steadfastness and by the encouragement of the Scriptures we might have hope' (Rom. 15:4)." We do not need "answers"—we need hope!

Bavinck continued,

> The doctrine of providence is not a philosophical system but a confession of faith, the confession that, notwithstanding appearances, neither Satan nor a human being nor any other creature, but God and he alone—by his almighty and everywhere present power—preserves and governs all things. Such a confession can save us both from a superficial optimism that denies the riddles of life, and from a presumptuous pessimism that despairs of this world and human destiny.

What should our focus be? We look for God's continuing involvement with the world and our lives to carry out God's divine purposes in Jesus Christ. We need this emphasis for the "big picture"—for believing that God enters into history to win the struggle against sin and evil, that God has the means to win, and that God means to win.

We need to believe every day in our lives that God is working out providential purposes for us. In faith, we trust God's guidance. We follow where God leads us in the way of Jesus.

**Reflection Point:** Consider ways you have seen God's providence at work in the world and in your life. Reflect on what God is calling you to do and be and the ways you can carry out God's purposes.

# Divine Providence

*Not the devil but God the Almighty, the Father of our Lord Jesus Christ, created the world. It is in its entirety and in all its parts the work of his hands and of his hands alone. And having created it, he has not let it go. He upholds it by his omnipotent and omnipresent power; he intervenes with his power in all creatures, and he governs and governs them in such a way that they all lead to and cooperate with his appointed end. God's providence, together with its maintenance and cooperation, takes up the third part of government. God rules; he is the King of kings and the Lord of lords (1 Tim. 6:15; Rev. 19:6), and his kingdom lasts forever (1 Tim. 1:17). Neither chance nor fate, neither arbitrariness nor constraint, neither capricious whim nor iron necessity, govern nature and history, the life and fate of mankind's children. But behind all secondary causes lies and works the almighty will of an all-powerful God and a faithful Father.*

# 19.

# Created in the Image of God

*So God created humans in his image,*
*in the image of God he created them;*
*male and female he created them. (Gen. 1:27)*

W HAT IS THE most basic thing we can say about human
beings? We may consider a number of things basic
to humanity—we live, we die, we have needs, we behave in
certain ways.

But isn't the most basic truth about us the conviction that
humans are created in the image of God?

This comes through in the first page of the Bible: "Then God
said, 'Let us make humans in our image, according to our likeness'" (Gen. 1:26). Humanity—all humans—are created in the
"image" of God (*imago Dei* in Latin). Bavinck wrote that "the
essence of human nature is its being [created in] the image of
God." This is the most basic reality of our existence!

Bavinck went on to say that the whole world reveals God.
Creation is a "mirror" of God's being—who God is. To some
degree, every creature embodies God's thought. But among the
world's creatures, only humans are "the image of God, God's
highest and richest self-revelation and consequently the head
and crown of the whole creation."

This is quite a word about us, isn't it? Imagine: only we humans are created in God's image. We bear this unique status—embodying the revelation of God's own self. In all dimensions of our lives, even in our sinfulness—our rebellion against God—we are still in the image of God. Humans are dependent on God, yet we live and act as we ourselves choose. We are an "immeasurable distance from God," yet intimately related to God. As Bavinck said, "How a puny creature can at the same time be the image of God is far beyond our understanding."

We can rejoice in being created in God's image. But our status in the whole of creation brings responsibilities. We are to use the gifts we have been given in service to God. God provides for us by putting us "over nature." But we are also responsible to our Creator: we are "under God." Rejoice and be responsible!

**Reflection Point:** In what ways are you conscious of being a living embodiment of the image of God? What kinds of responsibilities does this bring to you—and to the whole human family?

# 20.

# Humans *Are* the Image of God

*Then God said, "Let us make humans in our*
*image, according to our likeness, and let them*
*have dominion over the fish of the sea and over the*
*birds of the air and over the cattle and over all the*
*wild animals of the earth and over every creeping*
*thing that creeps upon the earth." (Gen. 1:26)*

I F HUMANS ARE created in the image of God (Gen. 1:26–30),
and if this is the essence of who we are, we wonder, What
does this mean? In what ways is living in the image of God
expressed in our lives?

In Christian theology, many suggestions have been made
about what the image of God means. Are we in the image of God
because we can use reason—like God does? Is our image of God
the "powers" we have that make us humans: rationality, dominion or sovereignty (over nature), freedom, or relationality?

Bavinck made it clear there are not just segments or "parts"
of our lives that constitute the image of God. Instead, Bavinck
wrote that "a human being does not *bear* or *have* the image
of God but . . . he or she *is* the image of God." The fullness of
who we are as humans is the image of God! Bavinck said, "This
image extends to the whole person. Nothing in a human being

is excluded from the image of God. While all creatures display *vestiges* of God, only a human being is the *image* of God." The totality of who we are as humans is being "the image of God." Nothing is omitted: not body, soul, or spirit. In all our abilities and talents and aptitudes, all our powers and conditions and relations—we *are* the image of God. Since we are truly and essentially human, we *are* the image of God!

Imagine the implications of this. Being the image of God gives us huge responsibilities. As some say, we are to represent God—like an image represents a reality. In who we are as persons, we represent—and present—God in every situation, every circumstance, every encounter we have. When people see us, they should see God.

We must also see others as images of God. They are created by God—and we are united with all other people by that fact. We care for them. The "human family" is a reality—we *are* the image of God.

**Prayer Point:** Pray that you may realize more fully what it means to be the image of God in who you are. Pray to see others as also being images of God and to care for them and love them as those who are created in God's image.

# 21.

# Original Sin

*All of us once lived . . . in the passions of our*
*flesh, doing the will of flesh and senses, and we*
*were by nature children of wrath. (Eph. 2:3)*

A N OLD SAYING tells us human beings are more like snowflakes than bottle caps. Bottle caps are all the same. But snow-flakes have differences—no two snowflakes are alike.

Theologically, there is a bottle-cap dimension to humans: We are all sinners. We are created by God, and "all have sinned and fall short of the glory of God" (Rom. 3:23). Sin is universal, and this unites the whole human race. Our hearts are evil (Ps. 51:5), and it is "from the human heart, that evil intentions come" (Mark 7:21).

The Christian doctrine of original sin does not mean we each have "original" or unique ways of sinning! It means we are sinful in our *origins* as the human race, as the Bible tells us in its Genesis 3 account of the human fall into sin in the garden of Eden. Theologians have seen sin as being rebellion against God, enmity toward God, and much else. This is the story of every person. We are sinful in our origins, and sin has spread through all who have been born since.

Bavinck's account indicates that "there is one human nature

common to all of Adam's descendants, and that nature is guilty and impure in all of them." This has consequences. Said Bavinck, "Original sin, into which mankind is received and born, is not a dormant, inoperative quality but a root from which all kinds of sins spring, an unholy fountain from which sin continually gushes like surging water, a force that always drives man in the wrong direction of his heart, away from God and his community, toward his own destruction and ruin."

The far-ranging nature and seriousness of original sin is indicated by Scripture. Humans are "dead through the trespasses and sins" (Eph. 2:1), making us "by nature children of wrath" (2:3). The human condition leads to death: "The wages of sin is death" (Rom. 6:23).

Only by recognizing the gravity of sin and what it means can we recognize God's amazing action: "The free gift of God is eternal life in Christ Jesus our Lord" (6:23)!

**Prayer Point:** Pray to God for the forgiveness of your sins. Thank God for the free gift of salvation in Jesus Christ. Ask God to keep you from the power of sin in your life. Work on not "explaining" your sin but confessing your sins.

## 22.

# Sin Affects the Whole Person

*You were dead through the trespasses and sins in which*
*you once walked, following the course of this world,*
*following the ruler of the power of the air. (Eph. 2:1–2)*

SOMEONE QUIPPED THAT after disobeying God (Gen. 3) our "first parents" said, "I've fallen and I can't get up!"

There is theological wisdom here. Sinful disobedience to God is serious—deadly serious. Sin affects the whole human race (Rom. 3:23), and sin leads to death (Rom. 6:23). The doctrine of original sin points to the wide-ranging effects of sin—for those who have come before us and for us as well.

Bavinck wrote that "as extensive as original sin is in humanity as a whole, so it is also in the individual person. It holds sway over the whole person, over mind and will, heart and conscience, soul and body, over all one's capacities and powers." Sin affects our whole selves. All dimensions of our lives are oriented by sin. The result is that all humans have a sinful nature, are corrupted from the image of God in which we were created (Gen. 1:26–30), and are inclined to evil.

Bavinck wrote that a human "by nature is totally incapable of this beatific good." We "cannot do any good that is internally and spiritually good, that is completely pure in the eyes of God." This is sometimes called *total depravity*. It means the totality of our lives are under the power of sin. We are helpless and powerless to do good in God's sight; as sinners, we are unable to will good but rather can only follow our natural inclination—which is to do evil. We are able to use our will: to make decisions and act. But the direction in which we will is toward evil and sin, not toward loving and obeying God or doing good. On our own, we do not want to do good. Our wills are corrupted by sin. We are "dead [in] trespasses and sins" (Eph. 2:1).

Theologically, this means we have no way to help ourselves to overcome sin's power in our lives. We cannot get up from our fall or pull ourselves up by our own bootstraps to overcome sin and do good.

Only God's power can save us!

**Reflection Point:** Think of examples of original sin you encounter or read about each day. Reflect on persons you know—and on yourself—who have received the gift of new life in Jesus Christ. In what ways can you reach out to those who live in the power of sin?

# 23.

# Idolatry

*You shall not make for yourself an idol. . . . You shall
not bow down to them or serve them, for I the LORD
your God am a jealous God, punishing children for
the iniquity of parents to the third and the fourth
generation of those who reject me but showing steadfast
love to the thousandth generation of those who love
me and keep my commandments. (Ex. 20:4–6)*

M ANY PEOPLE ARE concerned about atheism. They worry
about those who deny the existence of God.

But another danger is a bigger problem or evil: idolatry.

The second of the Ten Commandments says, "You shall not
make for yourself an idol, whether in the form of anything that
is in heaven above or that is on the earth beneath. . . . You shall
not bow down to them or serve them" (Ex. 20:4, 5). Throughout
the Old Testament, we see nations that worshiped gods as graven
images or idols—in animal or human forms.

The problem was not atheism. It was that they tried to cap-
ture or represent God by constructing some object or idea that
took the place of God. As Bavinck wrote, "Idolatry consists of
inventing something else in place of the one true God . . . upon
which man puts his trust."

Idolatry is a matter of the human heart. No wonder God's law forbids idolatry and warns against it!

Our problem with idolatry is persistent. We are always inventing something to take God's place—to become our god. These can take almost any form. Today, ancient statues or images are replaced by the "gods" of our inmost hearts and desires. Our drives for wealth, or success, or certain interests or practices, or sins can cause us to make idols of these things and worship them. We start with ourselves—with what *we* want to believe or do—instead of first looking to what our Lord God says in Scripture about how to live according to God's will and about what we should value in our lives. We domesticate God to fit our own wills and desires. We exchange infinite for finite—some form or action we control and cannot give up. We try to get control of God. Our loyalties are to our own interests and desires.

Jesus Christ is the end of these gods. Christ destroys idols. In Jesus, we see the wisdom and power of God, who created heaven and earth. Jesus is the model for our lives—what to value and how to live.

Worship the true God!

**Prayer Point:** Pray seriously for God to show you the idols in your life. Pray to be able to reject the desires, values, loyalties, and activities that are yours and not God's. Ask God to help you to destroy anything that stands in the place of the true God who is known in Jesus Christ.

# 24.

# Seeds of All Wickedness

*There is no one who is righteous, not even one;*
*there is no one who has understanding;*
*there is no one who seeks God.*
*All have turned aside; together they have become worthless;*
*there is no one who shows kindness;*
*there is not even one. . . .*
*The way of peace they have not known.*
*There is no fear of God before their eyes.*
*(Rom. 3:10–12, 17–18)*

W E HEAR TALK in the church about sin. We hear that all humans are sinners, for "all have sinned and fall short of the glory of God" (Rom. 3:23).

We realize we are sinners. We confess our sins in church services, and we confess our sins to God in the silence of our own hearts.

Looking around us, we see many examples of sin. In the world as a whole and among people whom we know—or hear about—we clearly see the reality of sin and disobedience to God. Theologically, sin is serious because it expresses our rejection of God in our lives and our active rebellion against the ways God wants us to live. Bavinck wrote, "In its principle and essence,

73

it is nothing less than enmity against God and a striving for supremacy in the world. Every sin, even the smallest, serves this end as a violation of the divine law, in the context of the whole." We rebel against God.

Bavinck went on to describe our sinful condition:

> The seeds of all wickedness lie in every human heart, and the more we grow in self-knowledge, the more we recognize the truth of the confession that by nature we are inclined to hate God and our neighbor, that we are incapable of any good and are inclined to all evil. But this evil inclination does not lead to evil deeds in all people to the same extent; on the broad road, all do not walk at the same speed and all do not make the same progress.

Our enmity against God is real and deep. It does not show itself equally or in the same ways among all people. But the stark reality of our broken relationship with God remains. We cannot do anything "good" in ourselves to come to God, and we are "inclined to all evil."

The first move from sin to salvation—to new life in Jesus Christ and a loving, trusting relationship with God—must come from God. Our Christian lives all began here.

**Prayer Point:** Give deepest praise and thanks to God for providing for your sin to be forgiven in Jesus Christ and for the power of the Holy Spirit, who gives you the gift of faith.

# 25.

# Trinitarian Salvation

*When the Spirit of truth comes, he will guide you into all
the truth, for he will not speak on his own but will speak
whatever he hears, and he will declare to you the things
that are to come. He will glorify me because he will take
what is mine and declare it to you. (John 16:13–14)*

THE EARLY CHRISTIAN church believed that the work of one
person of the Trinity is also the work of the other two persons of the Trinity. God is one God in three persons. Each of the
three persons is fully God. The three persons work together as
one God. But each of the three persons also has distinctive tasks
to do in order to carry out salvation. Most generally, Bavinck
said, "All things proceed from the Father, are accomplished by
the Son, and are completed in the Holy Spirit."

The church maintains we have a trinitarian salvation. The
Father, Son, and Holy Spirit are fully involved in the whole
"divine economy"—the plan of fully acquiring and applying the
salvation God has established.

Salvation is the divine work of the entire Trinity. In this, each
of the three persons receives specific tasks and carries out those
tasks. These are worked out in history and in the lives of each
of us. Said Bavinck, "The Father is the origin, the Son is the

Acquirer, and the Holy Spirit is the Provider of our salvation." The whole Trinity participates in salvation. In election, the Father originates and chooses those who will believe in Jesus Christ. In his death and resurrection, Jesus Christ provides salvation and reconciliation between humans and God, acquiring salvation. In the work of illuminating persons and giving the gift of faith, the Holy Spirit provides and applies salvation to the elect.

This technical theology is important for our Christian understanding and our Christian lives. To realize the whole Trinity carries out our salvation gives us confidence, assurance, and comfort. We can be sure the God we see and know in Jesus Christ is the same God who is also Father and Holy Spirit. The electing God is the God of Jesus Christ. The Holy Spirit, who is at work among us and within us, is the Spirit of God and the Spirit of Jesus Christ, and he leads us into all truth (John 16:13) and service.

Praise the triune God!

**Reflection Point:** Think of your Christian experience and ways you have been aware of the work of each person of the Trinity on your behalf: Father, Son, and Holy Spirit.

# 26.

# God Appears to Our Eyes

*The righteousness that comes from faith says, "Do not say in your heart, 'Who will ascend into heaven?'" (that is, to bring Christ down) "or 'Who will descend into the abyss?'" (that is, to bring Christ up from the dead). But what does it say? "The word is near you, in your mouth and in your heart." (Rom. 10:6–8)*

W E REFER TO God's becoming a human person in Jesus Christ as the incarnation. *Incarnation* comes from the Latin words *in*, meaning "in," and *carnis*, referring to flesh. The incarnation means the second person of the Trinity (the Son) "assumed flesh" or became a human being in the person of Jesus of Nazareth.

Bavinck well wrote, "The incarnation indicates that the divine, the eternal, the invisible does not hover above us at an unreachable height (Rom. 10:6–8), but has entered into the human, the temporal, and the visible, and now appears to our eyes in no other way than physically—in human form and in a human manner."

In Romans 10:6–7, Paul asked whether anyone can ascend to heaven "to bring Christ down" or descend to the abyss "to bring Christ up from the dead." The good news is *no one has to do that!* Why? Because "the word is near you, in your mouth and in your heart" (Rom. 10:8). That is, Jesus Christ is with us. He is near us and within us—because God has become a human person in Jesus.

Imagine! God—the divine, eternal, and invisible—is not far removed, up in the heavens at some "unreachable height." Amazingly, God has descended into the human world, into our time and space. As God in "human form and in a human manner," Jesus lived among us humans. Now we know God because God appears to our eyes. God descended into the arena of our human existence, living among us and showing us "God in the flesh"—God incarnate.

This is the greatest news. We don't need to muse and speculate about God. No. Now we see God in human form: God in the flesh, God in the man Jesus. The God revealed in Jesus Christ is the eternal, triune God. For us—and for our salvation—God became a person to show us who God is and what God is like. Look to Jesus!

**Prayer Point:** Give praise and thanks to God for being revealed to us in Jesus Christ. Pray, as you reflect on Jesus's words and life, that you may follow in the way of Jesus.

# *Jesus Christ*

*The Christ who appears on earth in the fullness of time is, . . . according to the description that the Scriptures give of him, not a man beside and in the midst of other men, not the founder of a divine service, and not the preacher of a new moral doctrine but occupies a wholly unique place. He was the Creator, Sustainer, and Ruler of all things; in him was the life and light of men. When he appears in the world, he does not come to it as a stranger, but he is its Lord, knows it, and is related to it. Re-creation is related to creation, grace to nature, the work of the Son to the work of the Father. Salvation is built on foundations that have been laid in creation.*

# 27.

# The Incarnation, a Wonderful Confession

*In the beginning was the Word, and the Word was with God, and the Word was God. . . . And the Word became flesh and lived among us, and we have seen his glory, the glory as of a father's only son, full of grace and truth. (John 1:1, 14)*

THE CHRISTIAN DOCTRINE of Christ's incarnation stresses the uniqueness of Jesus Christ. In faith, we believe the second person of the Trinity took on human flesh and actually *became* a person. Christ did not form an alliance with a person or draw an already human person into a community with himself. To do such a thing would mean Jesus was not a truly human person in himself.

Rather, the church believes Jesus Christ has two natures: divine and human. He is fully divine and fully human. The two natures exist together in one person. As Bavinck put it, "The union that came about in his incarnation was not a moral one between two persons, but the union of two natures in the same person. . . . Here is a completely unique, incomparable and incomprehensible union of God and man. The Word became flesh and dwelt among us, and we beheld His glory, the glory as of the only begotten of the Father, full of grace and truth (John 1:14)."

It is essential that Christ have two natures. For our salvation in his death, Jesus took on the sins of all humans: he is truly human. Jesus's death has the power to bring salvation because he is truly God. His death brought God's power to forgive sinners and reconcile them to God.

Jesus's "two natures in the same person" is a christological mystery. As Bavinck noted, this is a "completely unique, incomparable and incomprehensible union" of the divine and human. We do not understand *how* this is possible. But we do not need to understand; we need to believe! We confess our faith in Jesus Christ, believing that he is truly divine and truly human and that "God proves his love for us in that while we still were sinners Christ died for us" (Rom. 5:8).

Bavinck gave us this focus when he wrote that "the incarnation of the Word is not a problem that we must or can solve, but it is a wonderful fact that we thankfully confess, as God himself places it before our eyes in his Word." We confess Jesus Christ!

**Prayer Point:** Pray in great praise to God that our salvation does not rest on our understanding but on faith. Reaffirm your faith to God in prayer and ask for God's Spirit to lead you to express your faith in word and deed.

# 28.

# The Mystery of the Cross

*But he was wounded for our transgressions,*
*crushed for our iniquities;*
*upon him was the punishment that made us whole,*
*and by his bruises we are healed.*
*All we like sheep have gone astray;*
*we have all turned to our own way,*
*and the* LORD *has laid on him*
*the iniquity of us all. (Isa. 53:5–6)*

THEOLOGICALLY, THE DEATH of Jesus Christ on the cross is called the *atonement*. Christ's death marked the reconciliation of humans with God through the forgiveness of human sin. Only the death of the incarnate Son of God could bring this forgiveness and reconciliation.

The Scriptures describe the mystery of the cross of Christ in a number of ways. They refer to this mystery as the sacrifice of a lamb, atonement by a priest, vicarious satisfaction of a legal penalty, victory over the powers of evil, among other images. But one constant is Scripture's recognition that it was God's divine love for sinful humans that was the reason for Christ's death "for us" (Gal. 3:13).

Bavinck wrote of the mystery of the cross: "Here is the mystery of godliness, the mystery of divine love. We do not understand the vicarious [substitutionary] suffering of Christ, because we, being haters of God and hating each other, cannot even remotely calculate what love is capable of and what eternal, infinite, divine love can do." God's love for us as lawless, rebellious sinners is amazing beyond words. God's divine love can love us "while we still were sinners" (Rom. 5:8)—a mysterious love no human love can match.

Bavinck continued, "But we do not need to understand this mystery: we may believe it, rest in it, glory in it, and rejoice."

The cross of Jesus Christ stands before us as the mystery of God's redeeming love for human sinners. God gave Jesus to die so our sins can be forgiven and we can be reconciled to God. The hymnwriter had it right. This "love so amazing, so divine, demands my soul, my life, my all."

**Reflection Point:** Think of the various ways Christ's death is described in Scripture and reflect on the implications and value of the different images for your life of faith.

# 29.

# The Cross Is the Hand of Peace

*In him all the fullness of God was pleased to dwell, and*
*through him God was pleased to reconcile to himself*
*all things, whether on earth or in heaven, by making*
*peace through the blood of his cross. (Col. 1:19–20)*

THE CROSS IS the central symbol of Christianity. We see various kinds of crosses throughout our culture—from church steeples to necklaces. The cross reaches out in many directions.

The cross of Jesus Christ reaches in many directions too. In the outspread arms of the crucified, Jesus Christ reached out to embrace the world. His hands were holding the whole world in the love of God.

Jesus Christ in his cross has the power to unite many elements and peoples. Christ's cross reconciles, bringing peace. As we see in today's verses, only Jesus—fully God and fully human—could unite God and sinful humanity through his death. Only through Christ and his cross can peace and reconciliation between peoples and nations and groups be possible. Only the crucified Christ can break down hostilities and bring peace (Eph. 2:13–16).

Bavinck wrote, "In the Cross of Christ which is an offense unto the Jews and foolishness unto the Greeks; sin and grace, law and gospel, justice and mercy, guilt and forgiveness are united and reconciled. At that Cross, God and the world, Heaven and earth, angels and men, peoples and nations extend to one another the hand of peace. For by the Cross of Christ, God has reconciled the world unto Himself—not imputing her trespasses unto her, and, triumphed over all authority and powers." The cross—an instrument of hatred and destruction in itself—has become the means by which the world can be reconciled to God.

The cross is the hand of peace because, through Christ, sin can be forgiven. Through Christ, the authorities and powers that seek to divide people and draw them into sinful attitudes and behaviors can be defeated so they cannot hold us in their grasp again.

Christ himself is our peace. He has brought us relief. In the battles of sin and strife, Jesus Christ is our life!

**Prayer Point:** Pray to Jesus Christ in deepest, reverent thanks for his death on the cross for our sakes. Pray that reconciliation, peace, justice, and love—radiating from Jesus—will be realities for the world and its peoples. Pray to live in the reconciling love Jesus showed on the cross.

# The Work of Christ

*The whole life of Christ acquires for us a wholly unique significance and a surpassing value. It is one perfect work that the Father has commissioned him to do. It can be viewed from different angles and from different sides, and we must do this in order to obtain an overview of the content and scope of that work. But we must never forget that it is a single work; it encompasses and fills his whole life from conception to death on the cross; just as the person of Christ is one in the diversity of his natures, so also his work is one; it is God's work on earth par excellence. Yes, even more, it is backwardly connected with the counsel and foreknowledge of God, with his revelation among Israel and his guidance of the nations; and forward it continues in a modified way in the work that Christ is still accomplishing today in the state of his exaltation. It is a work that has its center in time on this earth but that arises from eternity, takes root in eternity, and extends into eternity.*

# 30.

# Joyful Tidings
# for the Whole Creation

*He is the beginning, the firstborn from the dead, so that*
*he might come to have first place in everything. For in*
*him all the fullness of God was pleased to dwell, and*
*through him God was pleased to reconcile to himself all*
*things, whether on earth or in heaven. (Col. 1:18–20)*

W HEN JESUS WAS crucified on the cross, we see the depths
of human sin. Humans participated in profound evil in
order to crucify the innocent Son of God. We see the mystery
of evil and of human suffering in the death of Jesus.

But Bavinck also says that "the reverse side is not absent. It is
true that the cross casts its shadow over all creation but so does
the light of the Resurrection." In his resurrection light, we see
the marvels of the gospel of Jesus Christ. For it is "precisely this
sinful world that is the object of God's love." "In Christ God was
reconciling the world to himself, not counting their trespasses
against them" (2 Cor. 5:19). In Christ, all things are reconciled
to God (Col. 1:20) and under him brought together in unity
(Eph. 1:10). Bavinck wrote, "It is impossible to express the thor-
oughgoing universalism of the Christian faith in words more

powerful and beautiful than these." For "Christianity knows no boundaries beyond those which God himself has in his good pleasure established; no boundaries of race or age, class, or status, nationality, or language."

This means that "the Gospel is a joyful tiding, not only for the individual person but also for humanity, for the family, for society, for the state, for art and science, for the entire cosmos, for the whole groaning creation." All creation can receive the good news of Jesus Christ!

The gospel of what God has done in Christ affects the totality of life in this world and beyond. Our whole human existence is affected by the gospel. Our responsibility, as believers in Jesus Christ, is to bring the gospel to bear on the totality of our lives. We must proclaim—and live in light of—the gospel in relation to all cultural and societal elements of life with which we are involved. We share the joyful tidings for the whole creation!

**Reflection Point:** Reflect on the many ways you recognize that the gospel of Jesus Christ affects the world and all human activities—including your own.

# 31.

# Christ's Resurrection Proclaims Our Acquittal

*No distrust made [Abraham] waver concerning the*
*promise of God, but he . . . gave glory to God, being*
*fully convinced that God was able to do what he*
*had promised. Therefore "it was reckoned to him*
*as righteousness." . . . It will be reckoned to us who*
*believe in him who raised Jesus our Lord from the*
*dead, who was handed over for our trespasses and was*
*raised for our justification. (Rom. 4:20–22, 24–25)*

IN THE NEW TESTAMENT, the death of Christ is intimately related to the resurrection of Christ. Paul wrote that Jesus was "handed over for our trespasses and was raised for our justification" (Rom. 4:25). The death of Jesus brought reconciliation between humans and God. The resurrection of Jesus brought our justification and our acquittal. As Paul wrote, "If Christ has not been raised, your faith is futile, and you are still in your sins" (1 Cor. 15:17). The resurrection of Jesus shows the power of God. Christ's resurrection brings the benefits of Christ's death to us.

Bavinck discussed this when he wrote that "because he had obtained the complete atonement and forgiveness of all our sins by his suffering and death, he arose and had to rise. In the resurrection he became himself and we were justified in him and with him; his resurrection from the dead is the public proclamation of our acquittal." No wonder the resurrection is so central to our Christian faith! The resurrection is the means for our justification, bringing salvation in Christ and proclaiming our acquittal—all the benefits of Christ's death are now ours because Jesus Christ is risen.

Bavinck said that "without the resurrection, the reconciliation effected by his death would have remained without effect and application. . . . But now Christ has been exalted by his resurrection as Lord, Prince, and Savior, who can make the acquired reconciliation part of us in the way of faith. His resurrection is both the proof and the source of our justification." We are acquitted of our sins and justified by faith through Christ's resurrection (Rom. 5:1). As Bavinck said, the resurrection is "the guarantee of our forgiveness and justification (Acts 5:31; Rom. 4:25)." When we think of the resurrection, our hearts are full of praise.

Put succinctly, Bavinck summarized that the resurrection is "a divine endorsement of [Jesus's] mediatorial work, a declaration of the power and value of his death, the 'Amen!' of the Father upon the 'It is finished!' of the Son (Acts 2:23–24; 4:11; 5:31; Rom. 6:4, 10, etc.)."

**Prayer Point:** Reflect on the meaning of Christ's resurrection for you and incorporate its meaning into a prayer to God in praise for the resurrection of Jesus Christ.

❖

# Jesus Christ Is Lord

*He that therefore shall call upon this name, the name of Jesus as Christ and Lord, shall be saved (Acts 2:21; 1 Cor. 1:2). To be a Christian, [one must] confess with one's mouth the Lord Jesus and believe with one's heart that God raised him from the dead (Rom. 10:9; 1 Cor. 12:3; Phil. 2:11). The content of the preaching is Christ Jesus the Lord (2 Cor. 4:5). So much is the essence of Christianity drawn together in this confession, that the name Lord with Paul becomes, as it were, a proper name, given to Christ in distinction from the Father and the Spirit. We have as Christians one God, the Father, of whom all things are, and we unto him; and one Lord, Jesus Christ, through whom all things are, and we by him; and one and the same Spirit, who giveth to every man in particular according as he will (1 Cor. 8:6; 12:11).*

*The apostolic blessing therefore prays for the congregation the grace of the Lord Jesus Christ, the love of God, and the fellowship of the Holy Spirit (2 Cor. 13:13). The one name of God explains itself in the three persons of Father, Son, and Spirit (Matt. 28:29).*

# 32.

# He Ascended into Heaven

*As they were watching, he was lifted up, and a cloud*
*took him out of their sight. While he was going and they*
*were gazing up toward heaven, suddenly two men in*
*white robes stood by them. They said, ". . . This Jesus,*
*who has been taken up from you into heaven, will come*
*in the same way as you saw him go." (Acts 1:9–11)*

I N MANY CHURCHES, Ascension Day and Ascension Sunday
pass by with hardly a notice. Ascension Day is forty days after
Easter, just ten days before the big Pentecost event at fifty days.
Still, the early creeds mention it. The Apostles' Creed says of
Jesus, "He ascended into heaven, and sitteth on the right hand
of God the Father Almighty from thence he shall come to judge
the quick and the dead."

The ascension marks the taking of Christ up into heaven
(Mark 16:19; Luke 24:51; Acts 1:2, 9, 11, 22; 1 Tim. 3:16). Jesus
ascended into the presence of God. As Bavinck wrote, Jesus
Christ, "after his resurrection and ascension, has the highest
place next to God in the entire universe." Christ continues his
work (John 5:17), which includes interceding with God for
believers (Rom. 8:34). This is of immense benefit to us—because
Jesus Christ acts on our behalf, our prayers have power in him!

Christ is forming the congregation of his people. We are being "formed into the body of Christ" and being "filled to the fullness of God." Imagine!

Even more, in his ascension Christ "subdued all enemies and made all angels, powers and forces subject to himself (Eph. 4:8; 1 Peter 3:22)," wrote Bavinck. For in the ascension, Christ "triumphs over all the laws of nature, over the entire gravity of matter. Yes, even more so, his ascension is a triumph over all the hostile demoniacal and human powers, which God, in the cross of Christ, stripped of their armor, exhibited in their powerlessness, and bound to Christ's chariot (Col. 2:15), and which now are carried off by Christ himself as captives (Eph. 4:8)." The triumph of Christ's cross was that "he disarmed the rulers and authorities and made a public example of them, triumphing over them in it" (Col. 2:15). So now, no evil powers—of any kind!—can have control or power over the world, or us. All hostile forces are captive to Christ. In his ascension, Jesus Christ "triumphs over the whole earth."

What immense help and confidence Christ's ascension brings us! Christ reigns from on high.

**Prayer Point:** Pray to Jesus Christ. Thank Christ for his ascension to the right hand of God; for his everlasting, ongoing intercession on your behalf with God the Father; and for subduing all hostile powers that would hold us— liberating us to be "filled to the fullness of God."

# Christ's Ascension

*His ascension was . . . his own act; he had the right and the power to do it; he ascended by his own power (John 3:13; 20:17; Eph. 4:8–10; 1 Peter 3:22). For in it he triumphs over the whole earth, over all the laws of nature, over the entire gravity of matter. Yes, even more so, his ascension is a triumph over all the hostile demoniacal and human powers, which God, in the cross of Christ, stripped of their armor, exhibited in their powerlessness, and bound to Christ's chariot (Col. 2:15), and which now are carried off by Christ himself as captives (Eph. 4:8). Peter expresses the same idea by saying that Christ, after his resurrection, ascended in spirit . . . to heaven, announced his victory to the spirits in prison, and took his seat at God's right hand, while the angels and powers and forces were made subservient to him.*

# 33.

# The Knowledge of Faith

*The works that I do in my Father's name testify*
*to me, but you do not believe because you do not*
*belong to my sheep. My sheep hear my voice. I know*
*them, and they follow me. I give them eternal life,*
*and they will never perish. (John 10:25–28)*

T HERE IS A tremendous difference between knowing about
God and knowing God.

Lots of philosophies, theologies, and speculations can speak
about "God"—in some form or fashion. They would claim to
know about God.

Christian theology, according to Bavinck, is "the science that
derives the knowledge of God from his revelation, contemplates
it under the guidance of his Spirit, and then seeks to describe
it to his glory." In Christian faith, our knowledge of who God
is comes from God's revelation in Scripture. Scripture is read
under the guidance of God's Spirit. Our knowledge of God is
"not the fruit of intellectual investigation and reflection but of
childlike and simple faith, of that faith that is not only a sure
knowledge but also a firm trust that not only others, but also
I, have been granted forgiveness of sins, eternal righteousness,
and salvation by God, through pure grace, solely for the merit

of Christ's will." Our knowledge of God in faith is not what we "know about God" but an actual knowledge of God. It is a personal trust-knowledge that affects our lives.

We do not reason our way toward belief that a God exists. In Scripture we find examples of those who acknowledge a "God" exists—but who do not trust or obey God. Mere knowledge about God is not enough: "You believe that God is one; you do well. Even the demons believe—and shudder" (James 2:19); "Not everyone who says to me, 'Lord, Lord,' will enter the kingdom of heaven, but only the one who does the will of my Father in heaven" (Matt. 7:21).

Faith means more than knowledge; "to know God does not consist in knowing much about God, but it lies in the fact that we have seen him ourselves in the face of Christ, that we have met him on our path of life, and have personally become acquainted with his virtues, his righteousness and holiness, his mercy and grace in the experience of our souls." Jesus said, "My sheep hear my voice. I know them, and they follow me" (John 10:27).

**Prayer Point:** Thank God you hear the voice of Jesus Christ and are given the gift of the knowledge of faith. Pray for deeper ways of knowing God as you read Scripture, pray, and serve others. Deepen your knowledge of faith.

# 34.

# True Conversion

*You desire truth in the inward being;*
*therefore teach me wisdom in my secret heart.*
*Purge me with hyssop, and I shall be clean;*
*wash me, and I shall be whiter than snow.*
*Let me hear joy and gladness;*
*let the bones that you have crushed rejoice.*
*Hide your face from my sins,*
*and blot out all my iniquities. (Ps. 51:6–9)*

T HINK OF PEOPLE you have heard speak of their conversions. They often know the place and sometimes the exact day or hour when their conversion occurred.

In the New Testament, the most famous convert is Saul of Tarsus (Acts 9). On his way to stamp out the new movement of believers in Jesus Christ, Paul had a dramatic encounter with the risen Christ on the road to Damascus that struck him blind. When he regained his sight, "immediately he began to proclaim Jesus in the synagogues, saying, 'He is the Son of God'" (Acts 9:20). Newly named Paul, he became the greatest missionary for Christ in the early church.

Paul's was a true conversion. That is, Paul's life was forever changed after his encounter with Christ and his confessing Jesus

Christ as the Son of God. In his letters, Paul wrote about sin and faith and what it means to "walk in newness of life" (Rom. 6:4). Conversion means a turning around, a walking in the new life of faith that comes to us by God's Holy Spirit. In faith, when we become new people in Jesus Christ (regeneration), we live new lives in obedience to Christ as our Lord. We repent of our sin, not just deploring the "consequences of sin" but also, as Bavinck said, experiencing "an inner breaking of the heart . . . in a sorrow for sin itself, because it is contrary to God's will." As the psalmist prayed, "Hide your face from my sins, and blot out all my iniquities" (Ps. 51:9).

Conversion emerges from our being new persons in Christ in our new lives in faith. True conversion is "a heartfelt sorrow for sin" and "a hating and fleeing of sin," said Bavinck. Our conversion "is and remains a gift and a work of God, not only in the beginning but also in the progress." As Christians, we live out our conversion to Christ in our daily lives. God enables us to turn from selfish living to living for others and living—in all things—to "the glory of God" (1 Cor. 10:31).

**Reflection Point:** In what ways do you view your Christian life as a "converted life"? Do you remember a specific time and place at which you experienced faith and became a new person in Christ? Consider what difference your coming to faith has had and continues to have in shaping your life.

# 35.

# Justification in Christ

*We ourselves were once foolish, disobedient, led astray. . . . But when the goodness and loving kindness of God our Savior appeared, he saved us, not because of any works of righteousness that we had done, but according to his mercy. (Titus 3:3–5)*

SALVATION COMES BY God's grace as we receive justification by faith in Jesus Christ. God's Holy Spirit is

poured out on us richly through Jesus Christ our Savior, so that, having been justified by his grace, we might become heirs according to the hope of eternal life. (Titus 3:6–7)

This is a mouthful of theological terms, but they all are very important. In Jesus Christ, we are "acquitted of guilt and punishment," wrote Bavinck, and this is a "gift from God." For "Christ himself, in a word, is the righteousness with which alone we can exist before God (1 Cor. 1:30); he acquired by his suffering and death the right for himself and his people to enter into eternal life, free from all guilt and punishment, and to take a seat at the right hand of God." So "justification is therefore most certainly a gracious but also a righteous act of God, a declaration by which he as Judge acquits us of guilt and punishment and grants us the right to eternal life."

This means that "our comfort in justification lies in the fact that all the righteousness we need lies outside us in Christ Jesus. It is not we who must or can bring it about. But God reveals his righteousness in the gospel in that he himself provides righteousness through the sacrifice of Christ."

Our justification or salvation before God rests solely on what Christ has done for us—not on our own works but on the work of Jesus Christ. Christ has acquired eternal life for us—a new standing of faith before God—that begins now and lasts forever!

Our hope of eternal life is grounded in Jesus Christ our Savior (Titus 3:7). Christ's resurrection is "the guarantee of our forgiveness and justification (Acts 5:31; Rom. 4:25)," wrote Bavinck. Christ's resurrection is "the foundation and guarantee of our salvation." This is the strongest possible pledge and assurance of hope we can possibly imagine.

In justification by faith, our sin is forgiven, and we receive eternal life—all by God's grace in Jesus Christ! Praise God!

**Reflection Point:** Think of the wonder of knowing our salvation is grounded in our justification before God through Jesus Christ. Only the righteous Son of God could stand before God on our behalf and obtain forgiveness of our sins. Consider all the ways justification in Christ affects your life.

# New Life in Christ

*Sanctification of believers must be properly understood; it must not become a legal sanctification, but it is and must remain a gospel sanctification. It does not, therefore, consist in believers sanctifying themselves by means of a holiness that they themselves bring about new and for the first time or that does exist but that they must acquire by their own efforts and good works. The holiness revealed by God in the gospel is not only fully available in Christ but is also applied and worked out in our hearts by his Spirit. Paul says it so beautifully in Ephesians 2:10: "We are God's creation, created in Christ Jesus for good works, which God has prepared so that we may walk in them." Just as the first creation was brought about by the Word, so the re-creation receives its existence in the fellowship with Christ: believers are crucified, die, are buried, and are also raised up and reborn to a new life in the fellowship with Christ.*

# 36.

# Adoption

*God sent his Son . . . in order to redeem those who were under the law, so that we might receive adoption as children. And because you are children, God has sent the Spirit of his Son into our hearts, crying, "Abba! Father!" So you are no longer a slave but a child, and if a child then also an heir through God. (Gal. 4:4–7)*

O NE OF THE benefits of our reconciliation with God in Jesus Christ (2 Cor. 5:16–21) is that we receive "the remission of sins, adoption as children, peace with God, the right to eternal life and a heavenly inheritance (Rom. 5:1; 8:17; Gal. 4:5)."

Our "adoption as children" is based on God's declaration of redemption (Gal. 4:5) established in Christ. This becomes ours through faith: "In Christ Jesus you are all children of God through faith" (Gal. 3:26).

When our sin is forgiven, our guilt is gone. Our righteousness is declared in Jesus Christ, and we have peace with God (Rom. 5:1). At the same time, we are adopted as God's children who receive, wrote Bavinck, "the boldness to address God as their Father, and they are continually guided [by God] (Rom. 8:14–16; Gal. 4:6)."

The Spirit of God leads. This leading includes prompting us to pray and assuring us that our prayers are heard through Jesus Christ, the believer's intercessor with God (Rom. 8:34; Heb. 7:25). No greater privilege can be imagined!

Adoption as God's children is rooted in God's eternal intention: God "destined us for adoption as his children through Jesus Christ, according to the good pleasure of his will" (Eph. 1:5). God's covenant of grace includes our election as God's children. It is God's work that brings us into this new status before God through Jesus Christ.

We become heirs according to God's promise (Rom. 8:17; Gal. 3:29; 4:7). We look forward to a glorious future. God's children "expect with all creation the revelation of the children of God, the liberty of their glory, the adoption as children, namely, the redemption of their bodies (Rom. 8:23). Not until the resurrection of the dead, when the body will be completely redeemed, will the adoption of children be completed."

*Now* are we children of God (1 John 3:1)!

**Prayer Point:** Pray with deep thanks for your adoption as a child of God. Be grateful for God's election, redemption through Christ, and the Holy Spirit, who leads and guides you. Thank God for the heavenly inheritance that awaits the children of God.

# 37.

# The Church Is All Who Are Saved

*Since we are surrounded by so great a cloud of witnesses,*
*let us also lay aside every weight and the sin that*
*clings so closely, and let us run with perseverance*
*the race that is set before us, looking to Jesus, the*
*pioneer and perfecter of faith. (Heb. 12:1–2)*

C HURCH CAN MEAN many things to us. Communities are
marked by church buildings. We may think of the local
church building where we worship or of all the churches
throughout the world. We may think of Christians in our local
congregation or other fellow believers in Christ. *Church* evokes
a number of things.

In the Apostles' Creed, we say we believe in the "communion
of saints." This describes church. Bavinck wrote that "the church
is a fellowship or communion of saints. In its broadest sense,
then, the church embraces all who have been saved by faith in
Christ or will be saved thus." The church is people. They have
one thing in common: faith in Jesus Christ as their Lord and
Savior. This unites all as "the body of Christ" (1 Cor. 12:27). We
all confess Jesus Christ as God's Son, who died for our sins and

brings us into a relationship of faith with God. We are joined together in this common faith by God's Holy Spirit, who unites us in the church as God's people of faith.

In the church, we are "surrounded by so great a cloud of witnesses" (Heb. 12:1). This is a comprehensive view of the church. Included in the church are all who have been saved by faith in Christ or who will be saved. As Bavinck said, the church is "all the believers who lived on earth from the time of the paradisal promise to this very moment . . . [and also] those who will later, even to the end of the ages, believe in Christ." This is the greatest image of the "communion of saints" we can imagine. Many have gone before us in faith; we have sisters and brothers in faith today; and we anticipate new Christian believers still to come.

When we worship, we are linked with believers in Christ—past . . . present . . . and future! We do not worship alone. We are joined through faith with the "great cloud of witnesses" who surround us as church, "the people of God" (Heb. 4:9)!

**Prayer Point:** Pray in thanksgiving for Christian believers of the past, of the present, and of the future.

# 38.

# Perseverance of the Saints

*I thank my God for every remembrance of you, always
in every one of my prayers for all of you, praying
with joy for your partnership in the gospel from the
first day until now. I am confident of this, that the
one who began a good work in you will continue to
complete it until the day of Jesus Christ. (Phil. 1:3–6)*

C AN CHRISTIANS LOSE their salvation? After one has become
a Christian, can that faith be lost? A term for this is *back-
sliding.* Can those who begin the journey of faith turn aside or
turn around and lose their salvation?

This has been a divisive issue in Christian churches. The
Arminian tradition teaches that faith can be lost. It views scriptural warnings against apostasy as showing this possibility; it
also looks to the example of people who have shown strong signs
of faith only to turn away and end life apparently without faith.

The Reformed tradition teaches the perseverance of the
saints. The emphasis on sanctification or growing in faith is that
it is God who is "at work within us" (Eph. 3:20) and that, as Paul
wrote, "the one who began a good work in you will continue
to complete it until the day of Jesus Christ" (Phil. 1:6). Jesus
himself said, "I give them eternal life, and they will never perish.

No one will snatch them out of my hand" (John 10:28). Those who are held in God's hand will not slip through God's fingers.

Bavinck believed that "doubts and uncertainties come to an end if the endurance of the saints is not an act of man's will but a work of God that is accomplished by him from beginning to end; if, in other words, it is a preservation of God before it becomes the endurance of man." God's Holy Spirit works in the lives of believers "in such a way that they themselves also persevere in the grace given to them by God." God's faithfulness ensures this perseverance as well as salvation itself.

Bavinck wrote that some say "faith in the preservation of God should make true believers haughty and careless, but, on the contrary, it is a true root of humility, filial fear, true godliness, endurance in all battles, fervent prayers, steadfastness in the cross and in the confession of the truth, as well as firm joy in God." This is the testimony—and practice—of Christian believers. Deepest thankfulness for salvation in Christ leads to "the fruits of gratitude."

> **Reflection Point:** Think of people you have known who started out in faith but then seemed to fall away and never return. As you contemplate your own faith, what makes you sure it is God who holds you in perseverance and not your own efforts that enable you to continue as a Christian believer?

# Sanctification through Christ

*The holiness that we must partake of is . . . fully available to us in Christ. There are many Christians who, at least in the practice of life, think differently about this. They acknowledge that they are justified by the righteousness that Christ has wrought, but they pretend or act as if they were to be sanctified by a holiness that they themselves had to work out. If that were the case, contrary to the apostolic testimony (Rom. 6:14; Gal. 4:31; 5:1, 13), we would not be living under grace and freedom but still under the law. Gospel sanctification, however, is as distinct from legal sanctification as the righteousness of God revealed in the gospel differs from that required by the law, not in content, but in manner of communication. It consists in God granting us in Christ, with righteousness, also perfect holiness, and communicating it to us inwardly through the regenerating and renewing action of the Holy Spirit.*

# 39.

# The Savior and Judge of the Church

*Just as it is appointed for mortals to die once and
after that the judgment, so Christ, having been
offered once to bear the sins of many, will appear a
second time, not to deal with sin but to save those
who are eagerly waiting for him. (Heb. 9:27–28)*

A s WE LOOK to the future, we can anticipate the return of
Jesus Christ. Hebrews says, "Christ, having been offered
once to bear the sins of many, will appear a second time, not
to deal with sin but to save those who are eagerly waiting for
him" (Heb. 9:28).

Bavinck wrote, "That will be a tremendous event, when
Christ, sent by the Father (Acts 3:20; 1 Tim. 6:15), will appear
on the clouds of heaven; just as he was taken up into heaven
when he left the earth, so he will return from heaven to earth
at his return (Phil. 3:20)." For, as Bavinck noted, "he appeared
the first time on earth in the form of a servant, but he comes
back the second time with great power and glory (Matt. 24:30)."

When preachers talk about the second coming of Christ, they
frequently describe pictures of fear and judgment. Certainly a

coming judgment is real, as the Apostles' Creed says Jesus will "judge the quick [living] and the dead."

But Bavinck is right to say that "this *maranatha* [Hebrew for "Our Lord, come!"; see 1 Cor. 16:22] is the consolation of the congregation [comfort of the church]; he, who loved her from eternity and gave himself up for her in death, will come again to take her to himself and share her eternally in his glory. Her Saviour and her Judge are one and the same person."

We can eagerly anticipate the second coming of Christ when we realize our Judge is also our Savior! The early church awaited Christ's coming again as a "blessed hope": "We wait for the blessed hope and the manifestation of the glory of our great God and Savior, Jesus Christ" (Titus 2:13). The Christ who returns is the Christ who came to show God's love, to die for our sins, and to provide the way of eternal salvation. The One who knows us best—sinful selves that we are—is also the One who loves us most! This is the great comfort for the church. We face the future glory with hope, awaiting our Savior and Judge.

**Prayer Point:** Ask God to help you to look to the future return of Jesus Christ with hope. Ask for help in living each day in expectancy and in full service to Christ, who is our "blessed hope."

# 40.

# The Book of Life

*Many of his disciples turned back and no longer went*
*about with him. So Jesus asked the twelve, "Do you*
*also wish to go away?" Simon Peter answered him,*
*"Lord, to whom can we go? You have the words of*
*eternal life. We have come to believe and know that*
*you are the Holy One of God." (John 6:66–69)*

W E ALL LIVE . . . and we all die. What happens between
these two events is of eternal significance.

As we live, we need to be aware we won't live on earth forever.
We need help to face the death that will come to us. Where do
we find help? How do we live? What guides our days? Where
do we put our energies?

The Scriptures are thoroughly realistic about life *and* death.
Bavinck wrote an encyclopedia article on death. He noted that
in the Bible the whole person dies when the spirit or soul leaves
a person. Human death is not an annihilation but "a deprivation
of all that makes for life on earth."

But the Scriptures also proclaim that "our Savior Jesus Christ
. . . abolished death and brought life and immortality to light
through the gospel" (2 Tim. 1:10). We think of Peter's words to
Jesus: "You have the words of eternal life" (John 6:68). Through

the Scriptures, we know death is conquered by Jesus Christ in his resurrection. Death is not the last word . . . eternal life is ours through Christ, our Savior and Lord.

"This everlasting life," wrote Bavinck, "is already here on earth presented to [us] by faith, and it is [our] portion also in the hour of death (John 3:36; 11:25, 26)." We live by the promises of Scripture, the greatest of which is that in Jesus Christ we hear "the words of eternal life" and that, by faith, we can receive these words as a personal promise to each of us. The Scriptures are the means by which the message of this gospel of Jesus Christ is brought to us. The Bible brings us "the wonderful words of life"!

So, Bavinck concluded: "Scripture is not the book of death, but of life, of everlasting life through Jesus Christ our Lord. It tells us, in oft-repeated and unmistakable terms, of the dreaded reality of death, but it proclaims to us still more loudly the wonderful power of the life which is in Christ Jesus."

**Reflection Point:** Think of the sweep of your life so far. In what ways are you preparing for death? What new directions, emphases, or commitments can enable you to live your "eternal life" more fully—now?

# 41.

# Every Knee Shall Bow

*Therefore God exalted him even more highly*
*and gave him the name*
*that is above every other name,*
*so that at the name given to Jesus*
*every knee should bend,*
*in heaven and on earth and under the earth,*
*and every tongue should confess*
*that Jesus Christ is Lord,*
*to the glory of God the Father. (Phil. 2:9–11)*

PAUL'S GREAT CONFESSION of Jesus Christ in Philippians 2:5–11 consists of two movements: Christ's humiliation and Christ's exaltation.

In verses 5 through 8, we see Christ, the eternal Son of God and second person of the Trinity, being born as a human person in Jesus, becoming a slave and servant to all, and dying on the cross.

But after Christ's death comes his resurrection, his ascension, and his exaltation at the right hand of God. Verses 9 through 11 tell us the certain future is the exalted Christ. He is the One at whose name every knee shall bow . . . and every tongue confess, "Jesus Christ is Lord"!

Bavinck wrote that "the history of the world therefore ends in unity of confession. One day, angels and devils, the righteous and the godless shall agree in the acknowledgment, that Christ is the only begotten Son of the Father and therefore the Heir of all things. Then every knee shall bow and every tongue shall confess, that Jesus Christ is the Lord." All the various peoples of the earth will join in one common confession. They will all bend their knees in worship and acknowledgement: Jesus Christ is Lord!

This common confession is not found within human history. Not all those created by God recognize God's Son as Lord of all or Savior of their lives. But the day will come when the entire human race will unite to join in praise of the humiliated and exalted Son of God as Lord of all.

Bavinck continued, "What a future, what a scene! The whole creation upon its knees before Jesus! And upon all lips the one . . . confession, that Christ is the Lord to the glory of God the Father!" For "it is not the punishment of the wicked that is in itself the final goal, but the glory of God, which is revealed in the victory of Christ over all His enemies."

We anticipate the day when "every knee shall bow"!

**Prayer Point:** Pray in great thanksgiving and praise for the certain day when all people will worship and confess Jesus Christ as Lord. Ask God to help you to live with that reality always before you so your whole life will confess Jesus Christ as Lord and you will live according to Christ's will.

# 42.

# God Is All in All

*"God has put all things in subjection under [Christ's] feet."*
*But . . . this does not include the one who put all things*
*in subjection under him. When all things are subjected*
*to him, then the Son himself will also be subjected to*
*the one who put all things in subjection under him,*
*so that God may be all in all. (1 Cor. 15:27–28)*

W HEN WE THINK about the future, it holds few certainties for us. We do not know what tomorrow (or today!) will bring, much less how history will end or what its final act will be. We live by faith, day to day, trusting the future will take care of itself.

But we do know one certainty that transcends all else. However history ends, we believe the final word or act of history is that God will be "all in all" (1 Cor. 15:28). We cannot imagine anything greater than this! The eternal God remains the eternal God. God's purposes for the world and human life have been completed. God has "put all things in subjection under his feet" (v. 27). Jesus Christ will "[hand] over the kingdom to God the Father, after he has destroyed every ruler and every authority and power" (v. 24; see also Eph. 1:22). All is accomplished!

Bavinck wrote that "when Christ has gathered His church, prepared His bride, completed His kingdom, He hands it over to the Father, that God may be all in all (1 Cor. 15:28). I will be your God and you shall be my people, that was the substance of the promise; and that promise is perfectly fulfilled in Christ, through Him who was and who is and who is to come, in the New Jerusalem (Rev. 21:3)."

All threads and cords of our lives have been bound together in the personal purposes of God for each of us. The big path of human history has been completed with all ordained events and actions having taken place. The "wonderful works of God" have been lived out, and their consequences eternally resound. Over it all now, God is "all in all."

If the final word of reality, of history, is the ultimate triumph of the kingdom of Jesus Christ and the sovereign rule of God, then it is key for us to know we are living as God wants. Knowing that who we are and what we do are congruent with God's will should be issue number one for us. Make God "all in all" in your own life . . . now!

**Reflection Point:** What effects does it have on you, for your everyday life, to realize what the end of history will be? In what ways does God's being "all in all" give your life in Jesus Christ direction, purpose, and joy?

# PART 2

# LIVING AS A CHRISTIAN

# 43.

# One Continuous Coming of Christ

*See, I am coming soon; my reward is with me,*
*to repay according to everyone's work. I am the*
*Alpha and the Omega, the First and the Last,*
*the Beginning and the End. (Rev. 22:12–13)*

MANY FOLKS HAVE a desire to visit the Holy Land. They want to walk where Jesus walked.

I confess this has never been a longing of mine. Theologically, the reason is that today we are actually closer to Jesus than people were when he walked the earth. Why? Because now—after Christ's resurrection and ascension—Christ is not limited by time and space. In his days on earth, only those who were physically near him could see Jesus. But now Christ is fully present throughout the world. By the power of the Holy Spirit, Jesus is "closer to his own" and "more closely associated with them" than at any other point. Now Christ is continually coming to us and continually with us as he works within us and among us in the church on earth.

Bavinck noted that "the time that elapses between his first and second coming is one continuous coming of Christ to the world." He is applying to the church, "through his Word and Spirit from the moment of his ascension," the benefits of his death on our behalf. This will be completed upon Christ's return to earth.

Now, said Bavinck,

the history of the world, which lies between Jesus's ascension and return, is one continuous coming of Christ, one continuous gathering of his congregation, one continuous subduing of his enemies. We often fail to see it, and we do not understand it, but Jesus Christ is indeed the Lord of time, the King of the ages; he is the Alpha and the Omega, the beginning and the end, the first and the last (Rev. 22:13). Because the Father loved the Son, he created the world in him, chose the congregation and destined all those who were given to him to experience his glory (John 17:24).

Now we experience Christ's glory. The Lord of History continues to come to us in our histories—minute by minute, day by day. Jesus is at work to carry out his purposes—for the church and for each of us.

We are always experiencing one continuous coming of Christ!

**Reflection Point:** Think of the ways you experience Jesus Christ in your life. Reflect on when you are most aware of Christ's presence. Consider ways you can be more aware of "the continuous coming of Christ" every day.

# 44.

# Amen! to All God's Promises

*For the Son of God, Jesus Christ . . . was not*
*"Yes and No," but in him it has always been "Yes."*
*For in him every one of God's promises is a "Yes."*
*For this reason it is through him that we say the*
*"Amen," to the glory of God. (2 Cor. 1:19–20)*

WE HAVE EXPERIENCE with promises made and promises kept—or not kept! We have *made* promises; some we have kept . . . and others we have not. We have *received* promises; some have been kept . . . and others have not. We rejoice in promises fulfilled. We are saddened—even despairing—when promises are broken.

We bring this human experience with us when we consider the promises of God. We can't help it. We hope God's promises are true and God will keep them. Yet we may fear having faith in them, given the times we have seen human promises fail.

But, as Bavinck wrote, "Faith says yes and amen to all of God's promises, embraces them and rests on them." God's promises are not human promises—subject to uncertainty about whether or not they will be kept. God is God. God can be trusted—more than any human. So in faith, we can surely say "Amen!" to all God's promises. We can embrace them and

127

count on them with full assurance that we can rest in them.

*When* faith does this, said Bavinck, and *as* faith does this, "it gives the believer the boldness to apply all God's promises to himself and to appropriate them for himself; it becomes a firm trust that not only others, but also I, have been granted forgiveness of sins, eternal righteousness and salvation by God, through pure grace, solely because of the merit of Christ."

As we experience God's promises to us, through all the zigs and zags of our lives, when we find God's promises are sure and can be trusted, then God's promises become very personal—all of them. Now we have the confidence, the "boldness" to apply all God's promises to ourselves. Now we can believe, in firm trust, that even *we* have received God's promises of the forgiveness of our sins and of salvation by God's grace. Now I can say "Amen!" to all God's promises—which are for me.

How do we know this? We see that in Christ God's promises have "always been 'Yes'" (2 Cor. 1:19). In Jesus Christ, we can say "Amen!" to all God's promises.

**Prayer Point:** Call to mind various promises of God throughout the Scriptures. Meditate on them and pray that God will show you how these promises relate to your life.

# 45.

# The Comfort of Election

*Set your minds on the things that are above, not
on the things that are on earth, for you have died,
and your life is hidden with Christ in God. When
Christ who is your life is revealed, then you also
will be revealed with him in glory. (Col. 3:2–4)*

WHEN WE THINK of the gift of our salvation that God
gives us in God's gracious election, we are filled with
gratitude and thanksgiving, praise and consolation. Knowing
our salvation is grounded in God's will—and not our own—is
great comfort. Our salvation originates in the "counsel of God":
"In Christ we have also obtained an inheritance, having been
destined according to the purpose of him who accomplishes all
things according to his counsel and will" (Eph. 1:11). As Bavinck
commented, "The love of the Father, the grace of the Son and
the fellowship of the Holy Spirit are fixed for the people of the
Lord in the eternal and unchangeable counsel of God. This
counsel of God is therefore also unspeakably rich in consolation."

The comfort of election is in God's will and counsel as God
gives us the gift of salvation. Bavinck explained, "Father, Son,
and Spirit together have conceived and established the whole
work of salvation, and it is they who carry it out and bring it

to completion. Nothing comes from man. All things are of, through and to God. And that is why our soul can rest in this with unshakable certainty; it is his will, his eternal, independent and unchanging will, that in the church mankind will be restored and saved."

Nothing can be more certain, more secure, or more comforting than God's eternal will and purpose. Our salvation does not rest on the unstable foundation of our human thoughts or emotions or actions. Salvation grounded in God's eternal election enables us to live in confidence and freedom in doing God's will. It is God who holds us secure, not the unsteadiness of our own fickleness or feelings. Our life is "hidden with Christ in God" (Col. 3:3) or, as Bavinck says, in "the eternal and unchangeable counsel of God."

There is a great comfort in election in proclaiming God's Word. We share the gospel of Christ with others, believing their response is the work of God. Their faith does not depend on how well we speak!

**Reflection Point:** Think about the ways it is important to you that your salvation does not rest on your own efforts but is held secure in God's electing grace.

# 46.

# Salvation Is All of Grace

*By grace you have been saved through faith, and this is*
*not your own doing; it is the gift of God—not the result*
*of works, so that no one may boast. (Eph. 2:8–9)*

ONE OF THE continuing questions in the history of theology relates to salvation. Is salvation wholly the work of God? Or is salvation all the action of humans who desire to be saved? Or are the two combined?

This question has been disputed since the early Christian centuries. Notably, the great theologian Augustine (354–430) believed the Scriptures taught salvation was completely the work of God. The Reformed theological tradition, of which Bavinck was a part, agreed with Augustine. So Bavinck wrote, "Grace is the beginning, the middle, and the end of the entire work of salvation; it is totally devoid of human merit."

Since human sin is so serious, the Reformed believe sin affects the whole human being. This means humans cannot gain any favor or merit before God. We are incapable of generating faith by ourselves because our sin turns us against God.

If humans are to be saved, it must be fully God's work within us. Only God's power, by the Holy Spirit, can give us the gift of faith in Jesus Christ. Through Christ, our sin is forgiven. God initiates salvation, God saves us in Christ, and God continues to hold us in salvation throughout our lives.

Bavinck emphasized that the "entire work of salvation" is God's work. We give all praise, glory, and thanks to God. Our sure salvation rests in God's grace. We do not—and cannot!—deserve God's loving grace to us. We cannot earn God's love by doing good works. This was the emphasis of Paul when he wrote that our salvation "is the gift of God—not the result of works, so that no one may boast" (Eph. 2:8–9).

Our salvation is grounded in God's work, not our own. God saves us and continues to hold us secure in salvation through our whole lives. When we sin, God forgives. Nothing gives us more assurance, hope, and comfort than knowing our salvation is God's and in God's hands—not our own! Praise God for the gift of salvation. Salvation is all of grace!

**Reflection Question:** In what ways is it comforting to you to realize your salvation is all of God's grace?

# Righteousness through Christ

*The righteousness which God bestows in Christ and with which we can only exist before Him is . . . in no way the fruit of our labour, but in a complete sense a gift of God, a gift of his grace. We are justified freely by his grace through the redemption that is in Christ Jesus (Rom. 3:24). God's grace is the deepest ground and the final cause of our justification. But this grace does not form a contradiction to God's righteousness but is closely related to it. After all, Paul repeatedly says that God's righteousness was revealed in the gospel (Rom. 1:17; 3:5, 21, 22, 25, 26; 10:3), and likewise John says in his first letter (1 John 1:9) that God is faithful and just to forgive us our sins and to cleanse us from all unrighteousness, and Peter in his second letter (2 Peter 1:1), that we have obtained faith by virtue of the righteousness of our God and Saviour Jesus Christ.*

# 47.

# God Actually Forgives Our Sins

*The LORD is merciful and gracious,*
*slow to anger and abounding in steadfast love.*
*He will not always accuse,*
*nor will he keep his anger forever.*
*He does not deal with us according to our sins*
*nor repay us according to our iniquities. . . .*
*As far as the east is from the west,*
*so far he removes our transgressions from us.*
*As a father has compassion for his children,*
*so the LORD has compassion for those who fear him.*
*(Ps. 103:8–10, 12–13)*

WE MAY THINK that trying to understand theology, or God, or some theological thoughts is speculative. When we try to wrap our minds around certain ideas, these thought exercises may seem removed from our everyday lives, including our lives of faith.

When Bavinck spoke of our salvation as grounded in God's counsel of election (Eph. 1:11), this may seem abstract. But Bavinck argued that the idea of our election is actually "full of life and action," for God's counsel or election is "not only a work of his mind but also a work of his will, not only a thought that belongs to eternity but also an omnipotent power that realizes itself in time." That is, what we say about God, on the basis of Scripture, is actually expressed in human life—our lives!

Take the idea of God's love. When God is "called Love," said Bavinck, this does not mean only that God "thinks of us in Christ with benevolence" but that God "also demonstrates this love and pours it into our hearts through the Holy Spirit" (see Rom. 5:5). What could be more practical—and blessedly beneficial—than that!

Even more, when God conveys that "the LORD is merciful and gracious, slow to anger and abounding in steadfast love" (Ps. 103:8)—that God is the Merciful One—Bavinck said, God "not only says this, but he also shows it in the fact that he actually forgives our sins and comforts us in all our woes." This is mercy and grace in action! We experience who God is by what God does. We say God is love, has mercy, is gracious—but we can also experience this when God forgives our sins and comforts us. This is the God we need, and this is the God we have.

Bavinck noted that "when Scripture speaks to us of the counsel of God, it proclaims that God himself fulfills and fully realizes that counsel." We can trust God to act in ways that express who God is—in all things and especially in God's mercy, forgiving our sins!

**Prayer Point:** Confess your sins to God. Confess what you have done and have left undone. Pray with deep thanks that God forgives your sin.

# 48.

# Forgiveness Is Erasing

*Wash me thoroughly from my iniquity,*
*and cleanse me from my sin. . . .*
*Purge me with hyssop, and I shall be clean;*
*wash me, and I shall be whiter than snow. (Ps. 51:2, 7)*

SOMETIMES WE HEAR someone say, "I'll forgive you, but I won't forget what you did."

We can understand the impulse here. The consequences of actions live on. In one sense, they will always be with us. But in what sense is there forgiveness if a person continues to circle back to a wrong that was done and keeps reliving it? If we take our cue from how God forgives us, we will not get trapped in "re-remembering" past offenses.

Bavinck wrote about forgiveness in relation to the reconciliation we receive from God and the forgiveness of our sins by our Lord. He said that "the forgiveness that comes after the reconciliation is so complete that it can be called an erasing (Ps. 51:3, 11; Isa. 43:25; 44:22), a casting behind the back (Isa. 38:17), a casting of the sins into the depths of the sea (Mic. 7:19). The atonement removes sins as completely as if they had never been committed; it drives out wrath and makes God's face shine with fatherly favour and pleasure upon his people."

Forgiveness is erasing. What if we adopted this image—and this practice—when it comes to forgiving others? It has been suggested that while it may be difficult to say one does not remember when one has been wronged, it is possible to remember the past in a new way—not as a continuing offense but as a past offense that now has no more power or control or ability to drive a wedge in a relationship. Maybe that is the best for which we humans can hope.

But God's forgiveness is a total erasing! The scriptural images are of a full deleting or expunging or removing of the offense. The atonement of the death of Jesus Christ is so full and complete and comprehensive that our past sins are over and gone. This is our only hope, isn't it?

We should all move toward this goal of erasing through forgiveness: we should forgive others as we have been forgiven.

**Prayer Point:** Ask God to forgive and erase all your sins. Ask God to help you to forgive others and to no longer hold their sins and wrongs against them.

# 49.

# Forgiveness Is Received by Faith

*"Forgive the iniquity of this people according to
the greatness of your steadfast love, just as you
have pardoned this people, from Egypt even
until now." Then the LORD said, "I do forgive,
just as you have asked." (Num. 14:19–20)*

W E ARE WELL acquainted with sin. As people of faith, sin
is still all too real for us. We deal with sin every day.

Throughout the Bible, we find many descriptions of sin.
Bavinck wrote, "Sin is called by different names; it is not only
called *sin* in general, but also *crime, guilt, apostasy, rebellion* and
is always committed in the last instance against God, against
the God of the covenant, and thus always bears the character
of 'violation,' a breach of the covenant." Sin is contra (against)
God, and to be in sin is the most serious situation imaginable.

But Bavinck went on to present the rest of the biblical message. He wrote, "For all these sins, however, there is forgiveness,
but not in such a way that Israel has to acquire it by [its] good
works or even by [its] sacrifices. For forgiveness is contained in
the promise; it is a benefit not of the law but of the gospel; it is

not obtained by sacrifice but only by faith (Ex. 33:19; 34:6, 7–9; Num. 14:18–20)."

God promised forgiveness of sins in a message for Israel: "I do forgive, just as you have asked" (Num. 14:20). God makes the same promise for believers in Jesus Christ, in whom there is now the forgiveness of sins (Col. 1:14).

For us, the best news imaginable—the greatest news we can hear—is that God forgives our sins. We are forgiven not on the basis of anything we can do or try to do—not on the basis of any good works. We can never do anything good enough to merit God's forgiveness for our sins by obeying God's law.

The best news is that our forgiveness comes by God's action. Forgiveness is in Jesus Christ. Forgiveness comes when we confess our sins and ask God in faith to forgive us our sins through Jesus Christ. God's promise is that "if we confess our sins, he who is faithful and just will forgive us our sins and cleanse us from all unrighteousness" (1 John 1:9). Forgiveness is received by faith. Thank God!

**Prayer Point:** Spend time in prayer recalling your sins against God and against others. Express your sorrow for your sins. Ask God's forgiveness through Jesus Christ your Lord and Savior.

# 50.

# Forgive Us as We Forgive

*Pray, then, in this way: . . . Forgive us our debts, as we also have forgiven our debtors. . . . For if you forgive others their trespasses, your heavenly Father will also forgive you, but if you do not forgive others, neither will your Father forgive your trespasses. (Matt. 6:9, 12, 14–15)*

THE WORDS OF the Lord's Prayer fall easily from our lips. They are familiar and comforting.

In the prayer is the phrase "Forgive us our debts, as we also have forgiven our debtors" (Matt. 6:12). We know we need to pray for God's forgiveness, and Jesus authorizes this impulse in the prayer he gave his disciples.

But perhaps this phrase should give us pause to think.

To pray for forgiveness—and be forgiven—we are to believe God can and will forgive our sins. But along with this prayer comes a responsibility for us. We pray, "Forgive us our debts *as* we forgive our debtors." Our forgiveness by God for our "debts" (sins) is related to our forgiving others who sin against us. Bavinck wrote that these words "describe the attitude that must be present in the person making the prayer in order to receive, enjoy, and appreciate the benefits of forgiveness." Our attitude counts.

141

Bavinck continued, "Only then do we realize to some extent what it has cost God, in human terms, to grant us the forgiveness of sins in Christ, when we have rooted out all enmity from our hearts and forgiven our debtors wholeheartedly for all their sins. We can only pray for that forgiveness as a great and unworthy benefit with all the earnestness of our souls, if we are whole-heartedly forgiving our neighbor."

God forgives us in Christ—a forgiveness we do not deserve. When we pray to receive this forgiveness, we must have an attitude—and willingness—to forgive others who have sinned against us. We must forgive them "wholeheartedly for all their sins." We can seek God's grace in forgiving us only when we are committed to fully and completely forgiving others.

William Barclay said the word *as* here means "in proportion to." Our forgiveness from God comes to us "in proportion to" our forgiving attitude toward others.

Bavinck indicated that by grace God was willing to wipe out our sins. In receiving God's grace, we must forgive others fully and completely—because we have been forgiven!

May we forgive us as we are forgiven!

**Prayer Point:** Think of all those who have wronged you—and whose wrongs you are remembering. Ask God to forgive you for harboring an unforgiving attitude. Pray to God for forgiveness, and commit to forgiving those who have sinned against you.

# 51.

# A Personal Trust of the Heart

*We also constantly give thanks to God for this,*
*that when you received the word of God that you*
*heard from us you accepted it not as a human*
*word but as what it really is, God's word, which is*
*also at work in you believers. (1 Thess. 2:13)*

W HEN WE THINK of faith, in particular our personal faith,
lots of thoughts come to mind.

We know faith is not just "knowledge"—like a set of facts we
memorize in school or a list of reasons for some action.

When we think of Christian faith, we remember the Scriptures and what they represent. We think of the church and
what Christian people believe. We think of others we know
as Christians—those who live by faith and seek to be faithful
disciples of Jesus Christ.

Our faith must be personally appropriated. In addition to
speaking of the church's faith or the faith of others, we each
must speak of "*my* faith."

This means knowing the gospel message of Jesus Christ
is a message for *me*. We receive God's Word in Scripture as
being personally directed by God to *me*. As Bavinck said, "An
acceptance of that testimony with application to myself, a

reception of the word of God's preaching, not as the word of man, but as the Word of God (1 Thess. 2:13), a 'ministering' of the gospel as a message sent to me personally by God." The gospel comes personally to *me*. I assent to the gospel of Christ and accept Jesus Christ as *my* Lord and Savior.

The message of Christ is a personal message to me. In faith, I assent or confess that I believe the gospel of Christ is true. But, in doing this, I am doing more than just agreeing to a general truth or proposition. Faith is more than intellectual assent. Faith in the gospel, as Bavinck wrote, is faith in "something more and something else than a mere assent to the truth." Faith involves "the core of my being, in which my existence, my life, my soul, my salvation is at stake." The decision of faith is the most important decision we will ever make, for faith means "a personal trust of the heart in God's grace in Christ Jesus."

**Reflection Point:** Consider your life and ask yourself if you are viewing your faith as trust. For what are you trusting God? For what are you afraid or reluctant to trust? In what ways can your faith as trust be strengthened?

# 52.

# Being Forgiven Day by Day

*Pray, then, in this way:*
*Our Father in heaven,*
*may your name be revered as holy.*
*May your kingdom come.*
*May your will be done*
*on earth as it is in heaven.*
*Give us today our daily bread.*
*And forgive us our debts,*
*as we also have forgiven our debtors. (Matt. 6:9–12)*

SOME THINGS HAPPEN to us once; other things need to be repeated on a regular basis. We are well familiar with this pattern in our lives, so we can understand it also in our lives of faith.

For instance, when we come to faith in Jesus Christ, all our sins are forgiven. This is why "since we are justified by faith, we have peace with God through our Lord Jesus Christ" (Rom. 5:1). Our peace comes from God's full forgiveness in Christ Jesus.

But sin persists in our Christian lives. As believers in Christ, we are justified sinners. We still sin every day. So we continue to need forgiveness. We must "continually appropriate" forgiveness of our sins, "in order to enjoy the security and comfort" of forgiveness, wrote Bavinck.

"It would be easy," Bavinck said, "if we could walk according to the will of our heart with a 'once converted, remain converted' [attitude]." Then the need for continuing forgiveness would not be an issue. Many, Bavinck noted, "indeed continue to live on a past experience and reassure themselves with it." If we have been forgiven once or twice or more . . . some could assume that will cover all the sins they will commit into the future.

"But that is not the Christian life," Bavinck maintained. We need God's forgiveness day by day. Just as we pray for God to "give us this day our daily bread," so we must also daily pray the next petition, "Forgive us our debts, as we also have forgiven our debtors" (Matt. 6:12). We need forgiveness each and every day.

Bavinck wrote that "we only partake of the forgiveness of our sins, its truth and its certainty, in the long term, through the fellowship with Christ himself, in the activity of the sanctifying faith." Through our fellowship with Christ, we can approach God to forgive our sins. In Christ, our sin can be forgiven. But we need to confess our sin and receive forgiveness—daily!

**Prayer Point:** Make it part of your daily prayer routines to reflect on your life, remember your sins, and ask God to forgive you in Christ. Think too of others against whom you have sinned and seek their forgiveness as well.

# 53.

# A Seed in the Heart

*Those who have been born of God do not sin because*
*God's seed abides in them; they cannot sin because they*
*have been born of God. The children of God and the*
*children of the devil are revealed in this way: all who*
*do not do what is right are not from God, nor are those*
*who do not love a brother or sister. (1 John 3:9–10)*

W E REMEMBER JESUS'S conversation at night with
Nicodemus. Jesus told this leader straight up: "Very truly,
I tell you, no one can see the kingdom of God without being
born from above" or "born anew" (John 3:3).

We hear people say they have been *born again,* by which they
mean they have moved from death to life—from sin to salvation—or they have expressed their faith in Jesus Christ as their
Lord and Savior. Perhaps we remember a specific time or place
that would lead us to make that same confession. Or perhaps we
can say, "Yes, I have been born anew. But I do not know a specific
time or place when that happened. At some point, I confessed
my faith in Jesus Christ and a new life began for me."

Bavinck wrote about this: "The rebirth instills a principle
of new life, which the Holy Spirit creates in connection with
the resurrection of Christ, from whom he takes everything

(1 Peter 1:3). It plants a seed in the heart (1 Peter 1:23; 1 John 3:9) from which a whole new [person] arises." At some point, the Holy Spirit has moved us to faith in who Jesus is and what Jesus has done—for us personally. We have a "new birth" (1 Peter 1:3); we are born anew by an "imperishable seed" (v. 23). The Spirit has planted in the heart a "seed" that abides with us (1 John 3:9).

This experience of the Spirit—"being born from above"— brings a complete change in our lives. We now have "a principle of new life" grounded in the resurrection of Christ, said Bavinck, from which a whole new person arises! The imperishable seed of God's Holy Spirit is with us always. From now on, our lives are led and guided by the Spirit in obedience to Jesus Christ. We do not seek our own agendas for life, our own selfish aims, or our own unbridled ambitions and greed. We are now led by the Spirit. We now walk in "newness of life" (Rom. 6:4)!

**Prayer Point:** Pray to be aware of God's Spirit in your life, giving you new loves and leading you to serve Jesus Christ in new ways. In your prayer, rejoice and be thankful for the Holy Spirit, who lives within you.

# 54.

# We Receive the Holy Spirit

*All who are led by the Spirit of God are children of God. For you did not receive a spirit of slavery to fall back into fear, but you received a spirit of adoption. When we cry, "Abba! Father!" it is that very Spirit bearing witness with our spirit that we are children of God, and if children, then heirs: heirs of God and joint heirs with Christ. (Rom. 8:14–17)*

THE HOLY SPIRIT has sometimes been called the shy member of the Trinity. This is because in Scripture the work of the Spirit is directed toward Jesus Christ. The Spirit does not call attention to the Spirit but witnesses or points to Jesus Christ as God's Son: "Here is the Lamb of God who takes away the sin of the world!" (John 1:29).

The Spirit's work is to witness to Jesus Christ, and the Spirit does that in our lives. We are able to come to faith in Jesus Christ by the Spirit's witnessing within us, enlightening us, opening our eyes to see who Jesus is and what Jesus has done in dying for our sins. The illumination we experience is, as Paul wrote, the "Spirit bearing witness with our spirit that we are children of God" (Rom. 8:16). The Spirit gives us the gift of faith.

We receive faith by the Spirit, and we receive the Spirit in our lives as well. Bavinck explained that

> all believers receive the Holy Spirit immediately when they believe, even though their faith be ever so weak, even though they are anxious. That Holy Spirit is and remains a pledge, a seal of the future glory of such believers. . . . They are actually assured and sealed only when that Holy Spirit works so powerfully in believers that the believer knows infallibly: I am a child of God. I have the Holy Spirit, and in that Spirit I have the pledge of glory.

This is the blessed and astounding work of the Holy Spirit! We receive the Spirit as we receive faith—frail and weak though we may feel our faith to be. The Spirit is permanently with us, being "sealed" (Eph. 1:13; 4:30) in our hearts. The Spirit is the pledge of future glory that is assured and is "about to be revealed to us" (Rom. 8:18). The Spirit brings the infallible assurance that we are children of God (Rom. 8:14–17).

The Spirit works within us and among us in ways that we do not know. But we do know we have received the Holy Spirit . . . forever!

**Prayer Point:** Give thanks for the Holy Spirit and all the Spirit does in your life, in the church, and in the world. Ask to be more aware of the Spirit's activities every day.

# The Holy Spirit in Us

*The Holy Spirit is the great and almighty Witness to Christ, who takes up the cause of Christ in our hearts, leads us to faith in his name, and makes us know the things that are given to us by God in his Christ (John 15:26; 16:13–15; 1 Cor. 12:3; 2 Cor. 4:3–6, etc.). But this Spirit of Christ then makes us know the truth of God's promises and his faithfulness to us. But this Spirit of Christ also makes us know ourselves not only in our guilt and impurity but also in our fellowship with and participation in Christ. He also reveals us in our faith to ourselves. Having first convinced us of sin, righteousness, and judgment and having worked faith in us as the Spirit of faith (2 Cor. 4:13), he then comes to assure us of our faith. He becomes a Spirit of adoption (Gal. 4:6), a Spirit as befits children and dwells in them (Rom. 8:15) and makes us aware [that we are children].*

# 55.

# Sealed with the Spirit

*For we know that, if the earthly tent we live in is
destroyed, we have a building from God, a house not
made with hands, eternal in the heavens. . . . The one
who has prepared us for this very thing is God, who has
given us the Spirit as a down payment. (2 Cor. 5:1, 5)*

W E COME TO faith in Jesus Christ and are united to Christ
by faith through the work of the Holy Spirit. Then what?
What about our assurance of salvation through the long haul
of our lives? There will be times when faith seems tough. There
may be times when our spirits have a power failure or when
we suffer an eclipse of God. Who or what can pull us through?

Bavinck reminded us that "believers are sealed with the Holy
Spirit as a pledge until the day of redemption (2 Cor. 1:22; 5:5;
Eph. 1:13)." For "the Holy Spirit, who is given to the believers,
who has planted the faith in them and constantly sustains it,
who testifies in them, who leads them, etc., is the Holy Spirit."
God's Holy Spirit initiates our faith and leads us through all life.
The Spirit "also serves as a pledge and guarantee for believers
that they will be preserved until the day of redemption and will
inherit heavenly salvation." This is a promise of God that we
know will be fulfilled! For, as Bavinck writes, "that Spirit will

never depart from them, but remains with them forever (John 14:16)." We can ask for no greater assurance than the abiding presence of the Holy Spirit, forever.

God's promise and our guarantee is that whoever "has that Spirit belongs to Christ, is his property (Rom. 8:19), and is preserved by him for eternity (John 17:24)." Our assurance of salvation is the seal of the Spirit. So "Christ in heaven and the Holy Spirit on earth guarantee the salvation of the elect and assure them of it in their hearts."

The blessed promise that we are sealed by the Holy Spirit of God can get us through all our troubles, sufferings, and disappointments. We are never alone. God's Spirit is always with us. The Spirit is always at work, leading and guiding, comforting and sustaining us. The Spirit now is the "down payment" (2 Cor. 5:5) of blessings and glories that are to come for believers. We are sealed with the Spirit now . . . and forever!

**Prayer Point:** Pray in thanks and gratitude for the seal of the Holy Spirit in your life. Praise the Spirit for being with you always, for guaranteeing your salvation, and for being with you forever. Pray to recognize the Spirit's presence and work every day.

# 56.

# An Incalculable Wealth of Blessings

*And the Word became flesh and lived among us, and*
*we have seen his glory, . . . full of grace and truth. . . .*
*From his fullness we have all received, grace upon grace.*
*The law indeed was given through Moses; grace and truth*
*came through Jesus Christ. No one has ever seen God.*
*It is the only Son, himself God, who is close to the Father's*
*heart, who has made him known. (John 1:14, 16–18)*

THE PROLOGUE TO the Gospel of John opens with the famous phrase "In the beginning was the Word, and the Word was with God, and the Word was God" (John 1:1). This tells us who Jesus Christ is. Then we read about what Jesus Christ did: "To all who received him, who believed in his name, he gave power to become children of God" (v. 12). Then we read an astonishingly wonderful statement about Jesus Christ: "From his fullness we have all received, grace upon grace" (v. 16). Imagine "grace upon grace"—what could be a greater blessing! Jesus brings us grace . . . and then more grace . . . and then more grace! Bavinck exclaimed, "The benefits that Christ bestows on his own people in his communion may very well be summed up under the single name of grace. But that one name then encompasses a fullness, an incalculable wealth of blessings."

Yes, riches of blessings are ours by the work of the Holy Spirit, who brings us to faith in Jesus Christ. In Christ, we receive "grace upon grace."

Bavinck went on to list some of these blessings. They began with reconciliation. Then come "vocation [calling], regeneration, faith, conversion, justification, remission of sins, adoption as children, redemption from the law, religious freedom, faith, hope, love, peace, joy, gladness, consolation, sanctification, preservation, perseverance, glorification," and so on. But Bavinck said that to sum them up is impossible since "there is actually no list of them." How could we ever summarize the "grace upon grace" we receive from Christ? We can't!

We can know, though, what the benefits we receive from faith in Jesus Christ in the church mean for us. We can know that the blessings "comprise everything that the congregation as a whole, and every believer in particular, has received, is receiving, and will receive from the fullness of Christ through all times, in all situations and circumstances, in prosperity and adversity . . . in life and death, on this side of the grave and hereafter for all eternity."

What an incalculable wealth of blessings is the "grace upon grace" we receive in Jesus Christ!

**Reflection Point:** Think of how Jesus Christ gives you "grace upon grace." Consider all of what you recognize as Christ's grace in your life. Resolve to be thankful for it all and to find ways to share Christ with others so they too may experience this wealth of blessings.

# 57.

# Our Meat and Drink

*[Jesus] fasted forty days and forty nights, and afterward*
*he was famished. The tempter came and said to him,*
*"If you are the Son of God, command these stones to*
*become loaves of bread." But he answered, "It is written,*
*'One does not live by bread alone, but by every word*
*that comes from the mouth of God.'" (Matt. 4:2–4)*

W HEN JESUS WAS tempted in the wilderness (Matt. 4:1–11),
one decision he would make was most important: Would
Jesus remain faithful to God or give in to the temptations posed
by the devil?

After forty days and nights of fasting, Jesus was famished.
Then the devil came to him and tempted him by telling him to
command the stones around him to "become loaves of bread."
But Jesus said, "One does not live by bread alone, but by every
word that comes from the mouth of God" (Matt. 4:4; see Deut.
8:3). Jesus affirmed that his true nourishment for life—meat and
drink, as we say—did not rest in physical food alone but came
from the Word of God: what God says and reveals.

So for us. The Word of God, given to us now in Scripture, is
the source of nourishment for our lives. Every day! Scripture

conveys God's Word and will for our lives. Scripture forms the basis for our lives of faith as we seek to love and obey God.

Bavinck captured this when he wrote of God's Word that it "continually proceeds out of the mouth of God, that comes unto us in Christ, and that through the Spirit of Christ is declared unto our heart or conscience." We know this Word through the Scriptures, the Word of God to us. The Bible points beyond itself to the God who speaks in and through Scripture.

"Therefore," Bavinck continued, "that Word can be and indeed is the meat and drink of our spiritual lives. It is the medium, not the fountain of grace. God is and remains the giver and dispenser of all grace." Scripture conveys God's Word to us, so God speaks to us through the words of Holy Scripture.

Scripture sustains our lives. We hear God's Word in Jesus Christ (John 1:1) by the power of the Holy Spirit. Be nourished by Scripture!

**Reflection Point:** Contemplate ways in which Scripture functions in your life. In what ways do the Scriptures nourish you? In what ways do they provide your foundation for living? How does the Bible bring you to the "fountain of grace"?

# 58.

# Confessing Jesus Christ

*For one believes with the heart, leading to righteousness,
and one confesses with the mouth, leading to salvation.
The scripture says, "No one who believes in him will be
put to shame." For there is no distinction between Jew
and Greek; the same Lord is Lord of all and is generous
to all who call on him. For "everyone who calls on the
name of the Lord shall be saved." (Rom. 10:10–13)*

W HEN WE JOIN the church, we are confessing our faith in
Jesus Christ as our Lord and Savior. Different churches
ask various questions of those who are uniting with the church.
But a most basic question for all is "Who is your Lord and Savior?" The response is "Jesus Christ is my Lord and Savior." This
is a clear and compelling statement of personal Christian faith.

When Bavinck wrote about "the essence of confession," he
said that the original meaning of *confession* in Scripture is
"nothing else and nothing less than one's openly and publicly
testifying and witnessing of personal faith in Jesus as the
Christ." To confess is to affirm faith in Jesus as the Christ in
a public context. In this sense, confession of faith can happen in many ways, in many settings beyond that of a church
worship service.

Two features stand out, as Bavinck said. First, "confessing is a thing of the heart. It is rooted in the heart. It comes up out of the heart. It is a fruit of the faith of the heart." Without faith, no confession can be made, because "confessing is a thing of the heart." It is one thing to say we believe something *about* Jesus Christ intellectually. But true confession means we believe *in* Jesus Christ, because of who he is and what he has done.

Second, "the faith of the heart is not ashamed of itself but reveals itself in openly and publicly testifying and witnessing." One who believes in Jesus Christ in the heart *must* confess this faith. We must share our faith with others, formally and informally. No matter what their responses or what the consequences, we must speak our faith. "We believe therefore we speak," said Bavinck.

Paul wrote that "one believes with the heart, leading to righteousness, and one confesses with the mouth, leading to salvation" (Rom. 10:10). Said Bavinck, "Believing with the heart and confessing with the mouth therefore accompany each other, and belong inseparably together." Confess Jesus Christ whenever and wherever you can!

**Prayer Point:** Pray that God will open occasions for you to confess your faith in Jesus Christ—publicly and to others. Ask God for wisdom and courage as well as compassion and care as you confess your faith in Jesus Christ.

# 59.

# The Unbreakable Unity of the Church

*There is one body and one Spirit, just as you were called to the one hope of your calling, one Lord, one faith, one baptism, one God and Father of all, who is above all and through all and in all. (Eph. 4:4–6)*

CHURCHES ARE ALL AROUND US.

We are well acquainted with the varieties of churches that dot the countryside, stand on the streets of small towns, and nestle within big cities. We wonder about the history of each church sanctuary and its congregation. What binds all these many different churches together?

Along with all the apparent differences among churches and congregations, an unbreakable unity of the church transcends all else. Jesus pointed to this when he said to his disciples, "I am the vine; you are the branches" (John 15:5). All the "branches" of the church find their lives in the life of the "vine"—Jesus Christ himself. One of Paul's great images is that of one body united in one hope, as we saw in today's verses. In another place he writes, "There are many members yet one body" (1 Cor. 12:20).

The unity of the church is theological. The Christian church is rooted in the unity of the triune God. Father, Son, and Holy Spirit are three persons in one God: there is diversity and unity. We worship one God, who, by the power of the Holy Spirit, gathers together persons in the church to worship and serve Jesus Christ. The unity of the church is the work of the Trinity. As Bavinck put it, "The love of the Father, the grace of the Son, and the fellowship of the Holy Spirit are the part of every believer, of every local congregation, and of the congregation as a whole—and therein lies its deep, unbreakable, imperishable unity."

As we participate in local congregations, we need always to remember this "deep, unbreakable, imperishable unity" we have with other Christians in the communion of saints as we all worship the triune God.

Our unity in the church of Jesus Christ defines our identity as Christian people. Celebrate our unity in Christ with joy!

**Prayer Point:** As Jesus prayed for his disciples that "they may be one, as we are one" (John 17:11), so pray for the unity of the church of Jesus Christ throughout the world. Ask God to help you to promote ways that churches can work together in their common unity—to the glory of God the Father, Son, and Holy Spirit.

❖

# The Church

*The believer is never separate from himself and is never alone. In the natural world, every human being is born of the community of his parents and is therefore, without his doing, a member of a family, of a nation, and of all mankind. It is the same in the spiritual realm. The believer is born from above, of God, but he receives new life only in the fellowship of the covenant of grace, of which Christ is the head and at the same time the content. If by virtue of that rebirth God is his Father, the church may properly be called his mother. In the heathen world, too, no believer and no assembly of believers comes into being except by means of the mission that the church of Christ sends out there. From the first moment of his regeneration, therefore, the believer, without will or action on his part, is incorporated into a great whole, included in a rich community; he is a member of a new people and a citizen of a spiritual kingdom, whose king is glorious in the number of his subjects.*

# 60.

# Benefits of Baptism

*When they heard this, they were cut to the heart. . . .*
*Peter said to them, "Repent and be baptized every*
*one of you in the name of Jesus Christ so that your*
*sins may be forgiven, and you will receive the gift of*
*the Holy Spirit. For the promise is for you, for your*
*children, and for all who are far away, everyone whom*
*the Lord our God calls to him." (Acts 2:37–39)*

A S ONE OF the two sacraments of most Protestant churches,[1] baptisms often occur in church life. They consist of adult and infant baptisms.

Baptism has many dimensions. It is administered in the name of the Trinity: Father, Son, and Holy Spirit (Matt. 28:19). On Pentecost, Peter urged those on whom the Holy Spirit moved and worked to be baptized "in the name of Jesus Christ" (Acts 2:38). As the church developed and understood that Father, Son, and Holy Spirit are three persons and one God, baptism was carried out in the name of the triune God.

Baptism, said Bavinck, is "specifically a sign and seal of the benefits of forgiveness (Acts 2:38; 22:16), and of regeneration

---

1. The Lord's Supper is the other.

(Titus 3:5), an incorporation into the fellowship with Christ and his church (Rom. 6:4)."[2] Forgiveness of sins, becoming a new person (regeneration), being incorporated into fellowship with Christ, and becoming part of Christ's church—all these are wonderful benefits that baptism brings.

Bavinck also noted baptism is not only "administered to the adults who are won to Christ through the work of the mission but also to the children of the believers, for they are included in the covenant of grace with their parents (Gen. 17:7, 10; Matt. 18:2, 3; 19:14; 21:16; Acts 2:39), belong to the church (1 Cor. 7:14), and are included in the fellowship with the Lord (Eph. 6:1; Col. 3:20)." God's covenant of grace extends to believers and their children, those who share in God's covenantal love with their parents. Infant baptism thus witnesses to God's grace and to the widening fellowship of the church by the work of the Holy Spirit. Writing about the communion of saints, Bavinck memorably said that in the church "there are true believers present, if only among the babies in the cradle." As children grow, they can make personal, public professions of faith in Jesus Christ, affirming the promises made for them by parents when they were baptized as infants.

What appears to be a simple baptismal ceremony has meaning and importance beyond our imaginings!

**Reflection Point:** Think about baptisms you have witnessed and your own. Have you seen those baptized become active Christians? In what ways does remembering that you are baptized shape your life in Jesus Christ?

2. "Sign and seal" are images for sacraments favored by John Calvin. See his *Institutes of the Christian Religion* 4.15.1.

# 61.

# Members of His Body
# at the Lord's Supper

*The cup of blessing that we bless, is it not a sharing*
*in the blood of Christ? The bread that we break, is*
*it not a sharing in the body of Christ? Because there*
*is one bread, we who are many are one body, for we*
*all partake of the one bread. (1 Cor. 10:16–17)*

I N THE CHURCH, we participate in public worship and in the
church's sacraments, including the Lord's Supper. No matter
what form the Lord's Supper takes in particular churches, we
are making a public confession of our faith when we partake
of the bread and the wine. The church shares this Supper as a
body, together, as we see in today's verses.

We do not participate in the Supper because we are worthy
to do so. As those united by faith in Jesus Christ, we confess our
unworthiness to receive the grace of God in Christ in the Supper.
Bavinck wrote, "What a significant confession we therefore
make when we come to the Lord's Supper! We do not come to
it to testify that we are perfect and righteous in ourselves." Our
very imperfection and unworthiness lead us to the Supper to

receive God's gracious gift, given to God's people in need of forgiveness and continuing new life.

"Considering that we seek our life out of ourselves in Jesus Christ," Bavinck wrote, "we acknowledge that we lie in the midst of death. We confess in this sacrament that Jesus Christ is the true meat and drink of our souls, and that we are members of His body. For it is one bread, thus we, being many, are one body, for we all are partakers of one bread." Participating in the Supper is acknowledging that we are in constant need of forgiveness for our sins. We are members of Christ's body. Jesus Christ feeds our souls. With our sisters and brothers in faith, we are one in Christ Jesus. We are members of Christ's body!

**Prayer Point:** In your prayers, give thanks for the meaningful ways you experience the Lord's Supper in your life. Be grateful for the grace given to members of Christ's body and the ways the Lord's Supper can deepen your faith and strengthen the church community.

# 62.

# The Communion and Fellowship of Christ

*What we have seen and heard we also declare to
you so that you also may have fellowship with us,
and truly our fellowship is with the Father and with
his Son Jesus Christ. We are writing these things so
that our joy may be complete. (1 John 1:3–4)*

T HE GREEK TERM *koinonia* is rich. Among its meanings
are "fellowship," "communion," "close relationship," "participation," and "sharing." The term has theological as well as
personal dimensions.

The term is twice translated "fellowship" in 1 John 1:3: "What
we have seen and heard we also declare to you so that you
also may have fellowship with us, and truly our fellowship is
with the Father and with his Son Jesus Christ." The writer is
describing "the word of life" (v. 1) revealed in Jesus Christ that
is being shared within the Christian community. In Christ, the
community has fellowship with each other and true fellowship
with the Father and the Son. Their fellowship and communion
reflect a human and a divine relationship.

This participation in the lives of others as well as with God the Father and God the Son is a mark of the church. It is a divine/human relationship in Jesus Christ that binds the community together in a common life of love and care for each other.

Bavinck notes this relationship is shown in the sacrament of the Lord's Supper: "In the Lord's Supper is signified and sealed the communion and fellowship of Christ, which we, at all times, possess in the Word, and enjoy through faith. . . . As surely as we are true believers, we make confession of that faith throughout our whole life." The church community's communion and fellowship are enjoyed through faith. Faith in Jesus Christ binds the whole community together in fellowship—in a mutual sharing of and participation in life with one another. Fellowship in the church is permanent, as are communion and fellowship with Jesus Christ.

This *koinonia* is "signified and sealed" in the "communion and fellowship of Christ" that the church community experiences. In the Lord's Supper, we see this as a sign while the fellowship of the Supper takes place, and we know this communion with Christ is sealed in our lives by Christ's permanent presence with us.[1] Thank God for this *koinonia*!

**Reflection Point:** Consider the deep ways your life is enriched by the fellowship of the church. What do your personal relationships with fellow church members mean to you? Consider the deep ways your communion with Christ affects all aspects of your life.

1. "Sign and seal" are images for sacraments favored by John Calvin. See his *Institutes of the Christian Religion* 4.15.1.

# 63.

# Confessing Guilt

*Have mercy on me, O God,*
*according to your steadfast love;*
*according to your abundant mercy,*
*blot out my transgressions.*
*Wash me thoroughly from my iniquity,*
*and cleanse me from my sin.*
*For I know my transgressions,*
*and my sin is ever before me.*
*Against you, you alone, have I sinned*
*and done what is evil in your sight. (Ps. 51:1–4)*

A CORPORATE PRAYER of confession is found in many worship services. Reformed churches have stressed the importance of this time for all worshipers to confess sins to God in one voice. This prayer recognizes that all of us, in community, stand in need of God's forgiveness of our sin, and we acknowledge this by confessing our guilt together.

I once heard of a man who did not enter the church service until after the prayer of confession. When the pastor asked him why he waited until then, he said, "I don't commit the sins that are mentioned." We may think we are not guilty of those specific sins. But all Christians sin—and we all need to confess our guilt and be forgiven by God.

Bavinck wrote, "The true, upright confession of guilt is already a fruit of saving faith. For he, who in truth and humility confesses his sins, has certainly already sought the Lord, has placed himself before God's countenance and finds himself in the presence of the Almighty, and this he cannot do but in the belief that the Lord is merciful and gracious, slow to anger, and plenteous in mercy."

We confess our guilt to God because, in faith, we believe God forgives our sins in Jesus Christ. There is no hiding from God about our thoughts and actions. We confess in faith before God and ask, as the psalmist did, "Have mercy on me, O God, according to your steadfast love; according to your abundant mercy, blot out my transgressions" (Ps. 51:1), for "a broken and contrite heart, O God, you will not despise" (v. 17).

When we are sorry for our sins, we can come into the presence of God, confessing our guilt and asking for God's forgiveness. The promises of God are sure. So in worship services, the prayer of confession of sin is followed by a declaration of pardon in which we can receive and accept God's forgiveness. For "the LORD is merciful and gracious, slow to anger and abounding in steadfast love" (Ps. 103:8). Let us confess . . .

**Prayer Point:** Thank God for being merciful and for forgiving your sins in Jesus Christ. Confess your sins and guilt to God and ask God's forgiveness as you express sorrow for what you have done or have failed to do.

# 64.

# Hearty Repentance

*Now I rejoice, not because you were grieved but because your grief led to repentance, for you felt a godly grief, so that you were not harmed in any way by us. For godly grief produces a repentance that leads to salvation and brings no regret, but worldly grief produces death. (2 Cor. 7:9–10)*

THE BIBLE PRESENTS many definitions or pictures of sin. Sin is an act that misses the mark and departs from the way of God. Sin is rebellion against God. Sin is breaking God's law. It is injustice, disobedience, apostasy, guilt . . . and even more! In its essence, sin is "*contra* God"—sin is that which is against God.[1]

Sin cannot be explained or excused. Sin can only be confessed to God and repented of for the future. Bavinck indicated that confessing sin means acknowledging the "guilt of sin, because it displeases God and is in contradiction with His law."

Confessing sin must include "a hearty repentance." This is because "we have provoked God to anger with our sins, that we

---

1. This was a term used by G. C. Berkouwer, a successor of Bavinck and a theologian at the Free University of Amsterdam. See G. C. Berkouwer, *Sin*, trans. Philip C. Holtrop (Grand Rapids: Eerdmans, 1971). See also Bavinck, *Reformed Dogmatics*, vol. 3, ch. 3.

have sinned against His righteousness, yea more, that we have so grossly sinned against His love." Sin offends against God our Creator, the covenant God of love who is righteous and whose righteousness we have violated.

Even more, sin is a rejection of God's love. Sin is a deep wound for us because, in all ways, our sin stands against God and attempts to break the bond with God by which our lives are upheld. We see our sin; we look at God's love in God's Son, Jesus Christ. In sin we reject God's love and the love of Jesus for us. Bavinck noted that Jesus said, "If I had not come and spoken to them, they would not have sin, but now they have no excuse for their sin" (John 15:22). We have no excuse for sin; we can only confess our sin and repent from our hearts. Paul wrote that "godly grief produces a repentance" (2 Cor. 7:10).

To repent is to express deepest sorrow for sin and then to turn away from sin—to walk in a new direction in daily living. Hearty repentance can begin a new life!

**Prayer Point:** Consider your sins, past and present. In what ways have you experienced forgiveness for them? In what ways have you had a "hearty repentance" that has led you to move in a new direction?

❖

# Repentance

*According to the preaching of John the Baptist and Jesus, the kingdom of heaven is at hand. And both then proclaim that no attempt to keep the law or any zealous self-righteousness but only repentance and faith will open the way to that kingdom and its goods. To indicate this conversion, the Greek New Testament uses two words; the first . . . indicates an internal, spiritual change, a change in the moral disposition; the other . . . [indicates] the external change, the change in direction of life, that is the revelation and consequence of the internal change. In Acts 3:19, 26:20, both words are linked together: "Repent and be converted"—that is, change your mind and your walk, come to repentance and return.*

# 65.

# Dying and Rising

*Do you not know that all of us who were baptized*
*into Christ Jesus were baptized into his death?*
*Therefore we were buried with him by baptism into*
*death, so that, just as Christ was raised from the*
*dead by the glory of the Father, so we also might walk*
*in newness of life. For if we have been united with*
*him in a death like his, we will certainly be united*
*with him in a resurrection like his. (Rom. 6:3–5)*

REFLECTING ON BEING a Christian, we realize our lives are not the same now as they were before we came to know Christ. How different our lives would have been had we never been given the gift of faith in Christ. Here is a contrast. In whatever sense, we realize a difference between old and new.

The Scriptures see this old life and new life as the difference between those who live for themselves and those who live for God. This is a difference between unfaith and faith, between death and life (Eph. 2:1–7).

Paul drew this contrast in Romans 6 when he spoke of our "old self" that must be put to death in Jesus Christ so our "sin might be destroyed" and "we might no longer be enslaved to sin" (Rom. 6:6). Our "new self" (Eph. 4:24; Col. 3:9–10) comes when we are "buried" with Christ and—by faith—receive "new life" to enable us to walk in "newness of life" (Rom. 6:4). We become a "new creation" (2 Cor. 5:17).

Bavinck indicated the nature of our dying and rising, of the "old life" and the "new life." He wrote, "What is the death of the old [self]? It is a heartfelt sorrow that we have [provoked] God through our sins and that we hate and flee [God] more and more." In contrition and repentance, we hate our sins. We repent of them and flee from our sin "more and more." Our old lives were sin and death.

"And what is the resurrection of the new [person]?" Bavinck said: "It is a heartfelt joy in God through Christ and the desire and love to live according to the will of God in all good works." Rising to new life in Christ brings inexpressible joy. Christ becomes our all in all. The new self seeks to live as God desires, according to God's will—and loves to live this way! This exuberant joy is expressed in doing good works for God's glory.

Live your new life in Christ!

**Prayer Point:** Pray in gratitude for your new life in Christ. Ask God to remove any remnants of the "old life" that remain in your mind, heart, or actions. Ask for God's sustaining grace to help you to love living for Christ and to do things that bring God glory.

# 66.

# Saving Faith

*If you confess with your mouth that Jesus is Lord
and believe in your heart that God raised him
from the dead, you will be saved. . . . The scripture
says, "No one who believes in him will be put to
shame." . . . For "everyone who calls on the name
of the Lord shall be saved." (Rom. 10:9, 11, 13)*

W E SPEAK OF faith in different ways—all the way from
having faith in the brakes of your car to having saving
faith in Jesus Christ.

A quotation attributed to Mark Twain says "faith is believing
something you know ain't so." This may be what some think. But
for the Christian, faith is precisely opposite. Faith is believing
something you know *is* so.

Through Scripture, we come to a true knowledge of God
in Jesus Christ. By the work of the Holy Spirit, we believe that
Scripture is the Word of God and that Jesus Christ is the Son of
God, who died to save us. Both these dimensions are important. As Bavinck put it, "In a word, the faith to be saved is not
only a certain knowledge, a firm conviction, an unquestionable
certainty about the prophetic and apostolic testimony as the
Word of God, but it is also, at the same time, a firm trust from

person to person in Christ himself as the fullness of grace and truth, revealed by God in him. The one is inseparably connected with the other."

The Christ we encounter in the Scriptures is not just an idea but a real person. We can know Christ as Christ knows us. The Holy Spirit gives the gift of faith and a "firm trust" in Christ as we believe who Jesus Christ is and what Christ has done, particularly in dying on the cross and being raised from the dead for our salvation. Paul said, "If you confess with your mouth that Jesus is Lord and believe in your heart that God raised him from the dead, you will be saved" (Rom. 10:9).

Bavinck stressed that knowing and trusting God must go together: "Without knowledge no trust is possible, for how can we trust someone whom we do not know? But vice versa, if knowing does not lead to trust, then it has not been the right knowing; those who know the name of the Lord trust in him."

When we know Jesus Christ, we trust him. Saving faith knows and trusts Jesus Christ!

**Reflection Point:** Reflect on how different it is to think about Jesus Christ rather than knowing Christ as a real person. Think of ways your life has been changed—and continues to be changed—by your relationship with Christ.

# Mystical Union with Christ

*All these gifts . . . of forgiveness and renewing, holiness and glory come unto us through the Mediator, who hath earned and merited them with the price of His blood. They can only be our part and portion then, when we are participants of Christ's person. The mystical union with Christ precedes all merits and benefits and reveals itself first in faith and conversion. Even as natural life is granted unto us in birth and thereafter reveals itself in deeds of mind and will, even so spiritual life becomes our possession through regeneration or the new birth, thereafter to bear fruits of faith and conversion.*

# 67.

# Cooperating with God's Purposes

*Now to him who by the power at work within us is able
to accomplish abundantly far more than all we can ask or
imagine, to him be glory in the church and in Christ Jesus
to all generations, forever and ever. Amen. (Eph. 3:20–21)*

God is at work in the world!

We believe in God's providence. God preserves the world,
keeping it from falling back into nothingness. God supports the
world by working to accomplish God's purposes. God governs
the world as "King of kings and Lord of lords" (1 Tim. 6:15; Rev.
19:16), so God's ultimate reign will become a reality.

We live in the world God maintains. We seek to cooperate
with God to carry out God's purposes. We know God's power
is "at work within us" (Eph. 3:20). One of the great things about
God's providence is that God works through people—through
people like us, ragtag bunch that we are! God could accomplish
whatever God wanted in whatever ways. But the fantastic news
is God cuts us in on the action! God invites us to *cooperate* with
God so God's will can be done "on earth." This is immensely
exciting: cooperating with God!

Bavinck noted that God "intervenes with his power in all creatures, and he governs and governs them in such a way that they all lead to and cooperate with his appointed end." God works with people so that through what they do—in their freedom to act as they choose—God's work and purposes get done. This is amazing! As we and others make decisions throughout our lives, these decisions are part of God's plan and cooperation in the world, so God's aims and designs do come to pass.

One way of looking at this is to consider means and ends. The *ends* are God's purposes—what God wants to accomplish. The *means* are the "how"—the ways by which God works to carry out divine intentions. God's will for the world includes willing both God's ends and the means by which those ends are fulfilled.

This gives us great freedom! We can choose what seems best to us—in obedience to God. We can be confident and trust God to use our actions—and the actions of others—as the means to accomplish God's eternal purposes. Wow!

**Reflection Point:** Review your life and see the ways God has used your decisions and actions to accomplish what you perceived to be God's purposes. Resolve to become even more aware of the ways God is at work in your life and the lives of others.

# 68.

# The Foundation of Spiritual Life

*He who raised Christ Jesus from the dead will give
life to your mortal bodies also through his Spirit that
dwells in you. . . . If you live according to the flesh, you
will die, but if by the Spirit you put to death the deeds
of the body, you will live. For all who are led by the
Spirit of God are children of God. (Rom. 8:11, 13–14)*

T HE PHRASE *our Christian life* is helpful because it focuses
directly on our identity as Christian people and the kinds
of lives we seek to live. To focus on the nature of our lives
as they are shaped and formed by Christian faith is useful
because it gives us a sense of the trajectory and values our
lives embody.

Bavinck talked about the "foundational principle of the spiritual life." The triune God is the foundation of all life itself. The
psalmist wrote, "With you is the fountain of life; in your light
we see light" (Ps. 36:9). "Spiritual life" recognizes that our lives
from God are "spiritual" in their aims, content, nature, and
foundation. We are "spiritual persons." We are led by God's
Spirit (Rom. 8:14), who lives within us (8:11).

Bavinck saw that "the foundational principle of the spiritual life is the love of God in Christ poured out upon us through the Holy Spirit (Rom. 5:5)." The "love of God" is the "spiritual principle" by which our Christian lives receive their basis, direction, and inspiration.

God's love, expressed in God's covenants and in Jesus Christ, pervades the lives we live in obedience and fellowship with God. We can know that we are deeply loved and that God's loving care fills our lives every day.

We know God's love in Jesus Christ, who lived among us, fully human and fully divine, and who died for the sins of the world. Through Christ, "God was reconciling the world to himself, not counting their trespasses against them, and entrusting the message of reconciliation to us" (2 Cor. 5:19).

We know the meaning of Jesus Christ and his reconciling death by the work of the Holy Spirit, through whom "God's love has been poured into our hearts" (Rom. 5:5).

Our Christian lives are grounded in the work of the Father, Son, and Holy Spirit. The triune God is at work within us! Let us live by recognizing that God is with us.

**Reflection Point:** Consider how you want to live your life as a Christian person. Reflect on ways in which the work of each person of the Trinity—Father, Son, and Spirit—provides a foundation and direction for your living.

# 69.

# The Essence of Spiritual Life

*If we walk in the light as he himself is in the light, we*
*have fellowship with one another, and the blood of*
*Jesus his Son cleanses us from all sin. (1 John 1:7)*

MANY IMAGES ILLUSTRATE the Christian life. We may think
of what we believe as Christians. We may think in terms
of the ways we live. We may recognize our Christian lives in
terms of what we do, what actions we take.

Bavinck grounded the spiritual life in the foundation of the
triune God—Father, Son, and Holy Spirit. The implications for
Christian living emerge by the work of God and then shape and
direct the lives that we will live as people of faith.

Bavinck went on to explore the essence of the spiritual life:
the pervasive relationship we have with the God who gives us
life itself and also "new life" (see page 105) in Jesus Christ.

Bavinck explained, "Because love for God is its foundation,
spiritual life itself consists of fellowship with God, with Christ,
and with fellow believers. Love strives after and is fellowship, a
fellowship that is only possible through and in love." Fellowship
is the essence of spiritual life—our fellowship with the triune God
and also, relatedly, fellowship with each other in the family of faith
in the church (1 Cor. 12:12–31; Eph. 1:22–23; 4:16; 1 John 1:7).

The purpose of the Christian life—and of human life itself—is to live in fellowship with God. To exist in this relationship ought to be the goal of all humanity. Great intimacy of fellowship with God is possible for Christian people: we live in, through, and with the members of the Trinity. Those who do not live by this faith are "alienated from the life of God," as Paul wrote (Eph. 4:18).

Our fellowship with the triune God means we also have fellowship with others in the family of faith. Fellowship with others draws us into a communal life. The love of the three persons of the Trinity is shared in the lives of those who live "in God" and are committed to being "the body of Christ" (1 Cor. 12:27), the church. Where hate separates people from each other, love binds people together with each other as they are joined in fellowship with the triune God.

Christian life is fellowship. We share in the life of God and others!

**Prayer Point:** Pray for a deeper perception of what it means to live in fellowship with the triune God and to live in ways where this fellowship is expressed. Seek deeper fellowship with others in the church.

# 70.

# Imitate Christ

*Be imitators of me, as I am of Christ. I commend*
*you because you remember me in everything*
*and maintain the traditions just as I handed*
*them on to you. (1 Cor. 11:1–2)*

T HOMAS À KEMPIS (c. 1380–1471) wrote the devotional
classic *The Imitation of Christ* in 1418. In it, he sought to
instruct Christians to follow Christ as their model for living.

Looking to Jesus as the example to follow in our lives of
discipleship has always been part of the church's devotional
tradition. Paul urged his readers, "Be imitators of me, as I am
of Christ" (1 Cor. 11:1). Jesus's life became Paul's model, and
he urged the church to follow the pattern Jesus's life represents.

Bavinck also advocated Christ as the example Christian
believers should look toward in their spiritual lives. Jesus's
words and deeds guide us as we seek to be Jesus's disciples and
obey his command "Follow me" (Mark 2:14).

When we imitate Christ, Christ takes shape in our lives and
we "[enter] into permanent communion with him, particularly
in the fellowship of his suffering." We do not replicate Christ's life
or work, but we follow after Christ, imitating Christ in our own
ways. Christ takes shape in us through our own personalities,

our own callings. We shape our lives in accord with the life of the One who lives within us. Paul spoke of "Christ in you, the hope of glory" (Col. 1:27) and said, "You have died, and your life is hidden with Christ in God" (Col. 3:3). As Christ is in us, our lives are "hidden" with him, so our lives are to follow in the way of Jesus himself.

Because Jesus is the Son of God and we are God's children, we become "conformed to the image of his Son" (Rom. 8:29) as Jesus Christ lives in us. Bavinck spoke of the fellowship of Christ's suffering as a dimension of our fellowship with him. Self-denial and cross-bearing—marks of Jesus's life—will mark our own lives as Christ's disciples. Our ongoing personal communion with Christ will lead us to serve others and follow Christ, even when we must deny what is precious to us and even when we must suffer for others.

Imitate Christ!

**Reflection Point:** Think of the ways you are aware of living in fellowship with Jesus Christ. In what ways does the life of Christ shape your own life, and in what ways can you more closely imitate Christ in your daily living?

# 71.

# Test and Thermometer

*Take the shield of faith, with which you will be
able to quench all the flaming arrows of the evil
one. Take the helmet of salvation and the sword of
the Spirit, which is the word of God. Pray in the
Spirit at all times in every prayer and supplication.
To that end, keep alert and always persevere in
supplication for all the saints. (Eph. 6:16–18)*

PRAYER IS CENTRAL to the Bible. People who stood in
relationship with God throughout the Bible were people
who prayed to God. Most clearly, Jesus was a person of prayer.
Prayer is a means of communion with God and of conversation
with God.

Prayer is central to the Christian life. Among many admonitions to prayer is Paul's: "Pray in the Spirit at all times in
every prayer and supplication" (Eph. 6:18). Prayer is a core of
the Christian's life in communion with God in Christ and in
conversation with God about all things that arise—thus we are
to pray at "all times."

Prayer expresses our dependence on God. For Christians,
prayer is made to the triune God. Prayer expresses trust in God's
promises, is made in Christ's name and for the sake of Jesus

Christ, and calls on God for help in the face of all difficulties while expressing thanks for blessings and benefits received from God.

Christians firmly trust and believe that God hears and will answer their prayers (Rom. 10:12–14; James 1:5–7; 1 John 5:14). This trust rests on God's goodness (Matt. 7:11) and power (Eph. 3:20). The merits of Jesus Christ are a cause to trust that prayer will be answered: "If in my name you ask me for anything, I will do it" (John 14:14).

Prayer is one of the means by which God's will is carried out. Through prayer, answers to prayer emerge. So prayer is vital.

Bavinck wrote that "prayer is the test and thermometer of our spiritual life, its pulse, and the best medication for it (Matt. 26:41; Luke 22:43; Eph. 6:16–18)." Our prayers function as tests and thermometers because they indicate how lively our relationship with God is and the warmth of our devotion to the Lord: Do we practice prayer "at all times"? Do we turn to God in prayer often during the course of each day, or do we confine our prayers only to times of need? Prayer is our essential means of fellowship with God. Our praying is a test and thermometer of our faith. We need to "pray without ceasing" (1 Thess. 5:17).

Pray always (Luke 18:1)!

**Prayer Point:** Pray that God's Spirit will lead you to pray more often, to pray more deeply, and to pray with faith and trust that God will answer your prayers.

# 72.

# Comfort by God
# Leads to Good Works

*Now may our Lord Jesus Christ himself and God our
Father, who loved us and through grace gave us eternal
comfort and good hope, comfort your hearts and strengthen
them in every good work and word. (2 Thess. 2:16–17)*

WHEN JESUS WAS ASKED,

"What must we do to perform the works of God?" Jesus
answered them, "This is the work of God, that you believe in
him whom he has sent." (John 6:28–29)

Jesus was saying that faith is the one great thing the Christian
lives by and by which the Christian does the work of God.

Faith is primary. But what is the nature of faith, and what
does faith bring us? Bavinck wrote that "by its very nature, faith
brings comfort, peace, joy and happiness." These benefits of
faith cannot be attained in any other way, and they shape and
form us as Christian people.

But faith does not stop there. Bavinck went on to say that
"those who are comforted by God are afterward strengthened

by him in all good words and works (2 Thess. 2:17). Joy in the Lord is the strength of his people (Neh. 8:10)." The comfort of God leads to good works.

It's important to realize, as Bavinck said, that "the good tree precedes the good fruit; we do not live by but for good works." We are not saved by doing good works, but we are saved in order to do good works. What we do in service to God as good works in Jesus Christ emerges from our faith—the faith in Jesus Christ that brings salvation. Our salvation leads to good works of service to God and others.

Our Christian lives are full of activities through which we express our faith "in every good work and word" and do all things to God's glory (1 Cor. 10:31). We do what we do out of faith in Christ and our desire to follow in the way of Jesus. In speaking of the Christian, Martin Luther often said good works do not make a person good (saving that person). But a "good person" (who has received salvation) does good works. Our works are our faith in action. We do not take credit for or glory in our works and actions. We do things—great and small—to express our faith in Jesus Christ.

**Prayer Point:** Make it part of your prayer life to ask God to show you things you can do to express your faith and serve Jesus Christ. Be open, by the Spirit, to opportunities great and small.

❖

# God Arouses Us to Walk
# in Good Works

*Just like the sanctification, the preservation of the believers is applied and worked out in them by the Holy Spirit in such a way that they themselves also persevere in the grace given to them by God. God never forces but acts with man in a reasonable manner. In the rebirth he pours out new qualities and makes the will [actually desire what it did not desire before]. And in the same spiritual way he continues to work in the hearts of believers; he does not make them weak in a false sense but raises them up and makes them walk in the good works prepared for them. To this end he uses his Word as a means in his hands.*

# 73.

# Confessing through Service

*Come, you who are blessed by my Father, inherit the kingdom prepared for you from the foundation of the world, for I was hungry and you gave me food, I was thirsty and you gave me something to drink, I was a stranger and you welcomed me, I was naked and you gave me clothing, I was sick and you took care of me, I was in prison and you visited me. (Matt. 25:34–36)*

A N OLD EXPRESSION says actions speak louder than words. We know what that means!

The Scriptures speak of the importance of Christian actions as expressions of Christian faith. The book of James puts it clearly: "Faith without works is . . . dead" (2:26). Jesus's parable of the last judgment (Matt. 25:31–46) makes it plain that the way we treat others in need is the way we treat Jesus himself: "As you did it to one of the least of these brothers and sisters of mine, you did it to me" (Matt. 25:40). On the opposite side, "Just as you *did not do* it to one of the least of these, you did not do it to me" (25:45). As we serve others as individuals and the church, we serve Jesus Christ. We confess our faith in Christ by serving the needs of others.

Bavinck wrote about this. One "confesses in upholding and supporting the public service of the church, in acts of Christian assistance, in the supporting of Christian instruction, in the caring for the poor, in the visiting of the bound and imprisoned, in the clothing of the naked, in the feeding of the hungry, in the comforting of the weeping, in admonishing the unruly, in exhorting the disputers and unbelievers, in giving account of the hope which is in him, in keeping himself unspotted from the world." Whoever "believes, confesses." Our lives themselves become "a confession, a living, holy, God-pleasing sacrifice in Christ Jesus."

Serving others is not an option for us as Christians or as churches. It is an absolute necessity. Our service shows the genuineness of our Christian confession. Our lives become our confession. As has been said, we show the "genuineness of our 'be-lieving' through our 'by-living.'" We cannot bypass our commitment to meet human need in the name of a faith that is too narrowly focused.

Serving others springs from our love of Jesus Christ. We may need to widen our care and become more sensitive to human need so we can serve Jesus by meeting the needs of others.

**Prayer Point:** Spend time in prayer reflecting on the needs of those you know. Pray that God will open opportunities for you to serve them, no matter what hardships they face. Pray that the needs of others will always be a focus for your life.

# 74.

# Love for God

*One of them . . . asked him a question to test him.
"Teacher, which commandment in the law is the
greatest?" He said to him, "'You shall love the Lord
your God with all your heart and with all your
soul and with all your mind.' This is the greatest
and first commandment." (Matt. 22:35–38)*

FAITH AND LOVE are intimately bound up together. We may think of them as distinct—and they are. But in the Bible, they are related. Each one implies the other.

Bavinck put it this way: "Love follows faith; it is the echo of faith. In faith we receive, in love we give." He wrote this when discussing our duties toward God. These begin with the first commandment. Bavinck noted that Jesus spoke of it in today's verses when he said, "You shall love the Lord your God with all your heart and with all your soul and with all your mind" (Matt. 22:37; see also Deut. 6:5). Bavinck interpreted this to mean that "love for God is our highest duty; it is the virtue by which we love God as the highest and only Good. . . . God must and can be loved for himself alone [as the only true Good], and everything else in and because of him." All our love starts with God!

199

Our faith in God—who is known to us in Jesus Christ—means we love God. For Bavinck, "we love him precisely because he has given *himself* to us." This is the central conviction of our lives. We love God because God is God. God is the one worthy of our love, and we must give all our love to God. We are to love God with all that is within us. We love God as purely as we can because of who God is. God is the Lord our God, and our love for God envelops the whole of who we are as persons who have faith in God. Faith and love go together. Our love "follows faith"; it is an "echo of faith." We receive God in faith; we give love to God!

**Prayer Point:** Pray that you may grow in faith and love for God every day.

# 75.

# The Spirit of Love in the Law

*You shall not hate in your heart anyone of your kin;*
*you shall reprove your neighbor, or you will incur guilt*
*yourself. You shall not take vengeance or bear a grudge*
*against any of your people, but you shall love your*
*neighbor as yourself: I am the LORD. (Lev. 19:17–18)*

SOMETIMES CHRISTIANS MISTAKENLY think that the Old
Testament is a book of "law" while the New Testament is a
book of "gospel." This can lead to downplaying and neglecting
the Old Testament. It cuts apart God's revelation in history. God
was revealed to Israel and saved the Israelites by liberating them
from slavery in Egypt. So the Ten Commandments begin with
God saying, "I am the LORD your God, who brought you out of
the land of Egypt, out of the house of slavery" (Ex. 20:2). The law
that follows is presented in the context of the gospel—the good
news of what God had done for the enslaved people of Israel.

The whole spirit that motivates the law of Moses, the Ten
Commandments, and other Old Testament legal provisions is,
said Bavinck, "the spirit of love." Bavinck pointed out that Jesus
in the New Testament said the second commandment—to love
one's neighbor—is "equal to the first (Matt. 22:39), and in it the
whole law is fulfilled (Rom. 13:8; Gal. 5:14; 1 Tim. 1:5)." In Israel,

"this love is shown to the weak and miserable, the poor, foreigners, widows, orphans, servants and maids, the deaf, the blind, the aged, etc., in a mercy such as no ancient law knew." Israel's overwhelming concern was for those in need—all kinds of need. This was a pervasive part of Israel's faith. Bavinck believed this impulse surpassed that of all other nations in the ancient world.

Ultimately, God's law is motivated by the spirit of love. Paul captured this: "The whole law is summed up in a single commandment, 'You shall love your neighbor as yourself'" (Gal. 5:14). Christians who live by love are continuing to obey the command that God gave to Israel and that pervaded Israel's laws. Bavinck continued, "It has been rightly said that Israel's morality is written from the point of view of the oppressed. Israel never forgot [its] foreignness and [its] misery in Egypt."

In all our obedience to God's law, let us practice the law of love!

**Prayer Point:** Pray that God will help you to obey God's law and do God's will while powerfully motivating you every day to love those whom you can help and serve.

# 76.

# Continuing Christ's Compassion

*Come, you who are blessed by my Father, inherit the*
*kingdom prepared for you from the foundation of the*
*world, for I was hungry and you gave me food, I was*
*thirsty and you gave me something to drink, I was a*
*stranger and you welcomed me, I was naked and you*
*gave me clothing, I was sick and you took care of me,*
*I was in prison and you visited me. (Matt. 25:34–36)*

B AVINCK DEVOTED A section in his ethics to the topic of
"Love toward Those in Distress." This section is rich in
biblical examples of ways those in need are to be cared for and
love is to be offered to them. These include the "poor, the sick,
widows, orphans, strangers, prisoners," and others. In a mar-
ginal note to this section, Bavinck wrote, "People in distress
are of eminent importance in the field of ethics. They are there
in order that we lead others better to appreciate the benefits
that we have received from God . . . ; they are there in order to
teach us beneficence, compassion."

Bavinck's survey of Old and New Testament prescriptions for
the care of the poor is extensive. The Old Testament provides

for a Year of Jubilee (Lev. 25) and commands freely giving and lending to the poor (Deut. 15:7–8). New Testament concerns are for providing alms for the poor (Matt. 6:2), support for orphans and widows (James 1:27), and help for foreigners (Matt. 25:35) and prisoners (Matt. 25:36). In the early church, works of mercy were done by deacons (Acts 6).

The purpose of these forms of mercy, Bavinck noted, is "to heal and relieve human distress—a continuation of Christ as the compassionate High Priest. Mercy has its roots in a heart full of love." When we provide for the poor and those in distress, we continue to show the concern of Jesus, who had "compassion" on those in need (Matt. 14:14; 15:32; 20:34). Now the risen and ascended Christ is a "merciful" High Priest for all in need (Heb. 2:17; 4:15). We are granted the grace to participate in Christ's ongoing ministry when we give care and love to those in distress.

Our compassionate care is fueled by a heart that brims with love. In caring for those in need, we are being like Christ. We extend the love of Christ to those who are "the least of these" brothers and sisters of his (Matt. 25:40). Serving them is serving Jesus.

Continue the compassion of Christ!

**Reflection Point:** Think of ways you, the church, and others extend the compassion of Jesus Christ to those in need. Consider ways you can advocate and help those in need through social services and political actions as well as volunteering and helping neighbors.

# 77.

# Live the Life of Love

*I give you a new commandment, that you love*
*one another. Just as I have loved you, you also*
*should love one another. By this everyone will*
*know that you are my disciples, if you have*
*love for one another. (John 13:34–35)*

MANY THEMES MAY guide our Christian lives. Most likely, we draw these from the Scriptures: discipleship, obedience, service. All are important for followers of Jesus Christ.

But one theme stands out in the New Testament. Love. Jesus said it plainly: "I give you a new commandment, that you love one another" (John 13:34; see also 15:12, 17). Love for others is the mark of discipleship: "By this everyone will know that you are my disciples, if you have love for one another" (13:35). Paul picked this up when he wrote, "Walk in love, as Christ loved us and gave himself up for us" (Eph. 5:2).

Bavinck focused on this prescription for Christians. He wrote, "It is a life of love, which Christians must lead (Eph. 5:2), for it is the most of all virtues (1 Cor. 13:13), the bond of perfection (Col. 3:14), and the fulfillment of the law (Rom. 13:10)."

Paul placed love at the forefront of Christian virtues when he wrote that "faith, hope, and love remain, these three, and the greatest of these is love" (1 Cor. 13:13). We can give tangible expression to love. Bavinck noted that "one should practice love toward all, even one's enemies (Rom. 12:14, 17; 13:10; Gal. 6:10, etc.)." In this, we are following in the way of Jesus, who forgave those who crucified him (Luke 23:34).

Paul also wrote to "clothe yourselves with love, which binds everything together in perfect harmony" (Col. 3:14). Love is a "bond of perfection" because it draws together all things. Anything that does not spring from love or move into love is not what it should be. Love reaches out to embrace all and to bring all things together.

Love is also the fulfillment of the law. Paul said, "Love does no wrong to a neighbor"—and this is why love fulfills the law (Rom. 13:10). God's law forbids us from doing harm to our neighbors (all people). The law is fulfilled when we love others (Gal. 5:14).

Our guide for our Christian lives: "Live the life of love!"

**Prayer Point:** Make love a focus of your prayers. First, thank God for the love shown to us in Jesus Christ and throughout our lives. Then ask God to help you to love others. Ask for help to see those in need. Ask God to help you to show love to others in meaningful ways.

# 78.

# Neighbor Love to Everyone

*You were called to freedom, brothers and sisters,*
*only do not use your freedom as an opportunity*
*for self-indulgence, but through love become*
*enslaved to one another. For the whole law is*
*summed up in a single commandment, "You shall*
*love your neighbor as yourself." (Gal. 5:13–14)*

LOVE IS CENTRAL to the Christian life. Love comes from God because "God is love" (1 John 4:8). God has commanded human creatures to practice love toward one another. Bavinck wrote that "every human being is incomplete, onesided, and requires and possesses the supplementation of others. . . . The true relation of one human being to another is that of love. . . . That love is respect for and self-surrender to one's neighbor." Or, as Paul put it, "Through love become enslaved to one another" (Gal. 5:13). Paul continued, "The whole law is summed up in a single commandment, 'You shall love your neighbor as yourself'" (Gal. 5:14).

Paul's words, which echo emphases of Jesus (Mark 12:31; see also Lev. 19:18), call for a radical commitment to others—as humans and as "neighbors." Famously, when Jesus was asked, "Who is my neighbor?" he responded with the parable of the good

Samaritan (Luke 10:25–37). The one in need is our neighbor—our neighbor who must be loved.

Bavinck indicated this: "Scripture speaks of neighbor love. And our neighbor is everyone, no matter who and what they are, who needs our help; and we are *their* neighbor. . . . That person is a neighbor who has a need, of whatever kind, . . . and then we must not first ask if they belong to our race, nation, or religion, or if they are needy through their own fault, and so on." We don't get to choose who our neighbor is! Our neighbor is everyone—no matter who or what they are. Our neighbor is anyone with a need—a need God wills that we meet.

This call for neighbor love for everyone is grounded in God's love for humanity. All people are created by God (Acts 17:28), and God cares for all (Matt. 5:45). As sinful persons, we do not naturally love others—we are inclined toward hatred and disregard for others' needs. The Holy Spirit brings us genuine neighbor love that is grounded in faith in Jesus Christ (Gal. 5:6).

Practice neighbor love to everyone.

**Prayer Point:** Pray to God to open your heart to see all other persons as neighbors. Pray that God would help you to meet their needs in whatever ways you can and to seek their well-being. Pray for God's Spirit to give you a stronger love for neighbors.

# 79.

# Love for Neighbor

*"Which of these three, do you think, was a neighbor to the man who fell into the hands of the robbers?" [The expert in the law] said, "The one who showed him mercy." Jesus said to him, "Go and do likewise." (Luke 10:36–37)*

WE OFTEN THINK love is easy. We speak of falling in love—as though it "just happens." We have natural love for our families and friends. In love, we look out for the best interests of others, trying to help and support them in every way we can.

But what about loving those outside our close circle—such as our neighbors or even our enemies (Matt. 5:44)? These are people for whom we may not feel a natural affinity, even people we may not like.

Jesus's parable of the good Samaritan (Luke 10:25–37) tells of a man who was beaten by robbers. After two others passed him by, a Samaritan—a natural enemy to the Jewish people—treated the victim's wounds, picked him up, and provided for his recuperation at an inn. He showed love for his neighbor—and Jesus affirmed this action, echoing his command "You shall love your neighbor as yourself" (Mark 12:31; see also Lev. 19:18). Jesus concluded that we are to "go and do likewise."

Why is it not natural for us to love our neighbors? Bavinck wrote, "Love for one's neighbor is not something that comes naturally and spontaneously from the human heart. It is a feeling, an act, an activity that requires immense willpower and must be constantly maintained against the tremendous powers of selfishness and self-interest." It takes willpower—commitment—to show love for strangers, even enemies. We are naturally looking out for ourselves. To look out and care for others takes us beyond ourselves.

Bavinck continued, "Love for one's neighbor can only be sustained if, on the one hand, it is founded in and imposed on us by God's commandment, and if, on the other hand, that same God gives us the desire in our hearts to walk in sincerity according to all his commandments." God commands us to love our neighbors, so we should. But Bavinck affirms that God can also give us the desire to love our neighbors and care for them. We should always pray for God to instill love for neighbors in our hearts . . . and then practice it!

**Reflection Point:** In what ways do you find it hard to love your neighbor? What are ways you can become more willing—and able—to carry out Jesus's command?

# 80.

# The Value of the Whole World

*Do not store up for yourselves treasures on earth, where
moth and rust consume and where thieves break in and
steal, but store up for yourselves treasures in heaven,
where neither moth nor rust consumes and where thieves
do not break in and steal. For where your treasure
is, there your heart will be also. (Matt. 6:19–21)*

A s CHRISTIANS WE constantly evaluate the cultures around
us in their many forms. We learn about, consider, and
decide what elements of a culture we should use and what cultural activities we should participate in. We are surrounded by
many cultural forms, and so we need to ponder how they relate
to our Christian faith.

Many cultural considerations relate to our possessions. We
think about how to regard the things we own and the various
resources we have, including financial assets.

We are always caught up short when we read Jesus's words in
the verses for today's reading. We know we need certain possessions to live in our world. But Jesus warns us about investing our
hearts in our treasure—making our possessions and resources
the main focus of our lives. We need to keep our possessions
in perspective and keep our main focus on living as God wants

us to live. As Jesus went on to say, "Seek first the kingdom of God and his righteousness, and all these things will be given to you as well" (Matt. 6:33). Our main focus is God's kingdom.

Bavinck indicated this when he wrote, "Although the Christian religion is not at enmity with culture in principle, still there is no gainsaying that it attributes only a subordinate value to all the possessions of this earthly life. The value of the whole world is not so great as that of the righteousness of the kingdom of heaven, the forgiveness of sins, and eternal life in fellowship with God."

The value of the world cannot begin to be so great as the value of being forgiven and living eternally in God's kingdom! God's kingdom is our true treasure!

**Prayer Point:** Pray for God to show you the things in your life that are becoming too important as treasures. Ask God to redirect your values to seeking more clearly God's kingdom. Pray through what this might mean for how you live and for what you value most.

# 81.

# Nothing Separates Us
# from God's Love

*For I am convinced that neither death, nor life, nor
angels, nor rulers, nor things present, nor things to
come, nor powers, nor height, nor depth, nor anything
else in all creation will be able to separate us from the
love of God in Christ Jesus our Lord. (Rom. 8:38–39)*

W E ALL LIVE with doubt. To some degree, doubt is a constant companion. Some people are plagued by doubt
more than others and may feel paralyzed by it. Even through
the normal events of life, doubt raises its head. Life events can
shake us and cause us to question aspects of our Christian
faith—or even our faith itself.

Bavinck recognized this when he wrote that for some "faith
in the providence of God was . . . shaken by doubt, and [they]
often proved unable to withstand the vicissitudes of life." For
example, when "the city of Lisbon was largely destroyed by a
terrible earthquake in 1755, many began to blaspheme God's
providence and to deny his existence." When life tumbles in,
can we continue to believe in God's love?

As we see in our verses today, Paul's answer was resounding. Paul's words in Romans 8:38–39 are a supreme claim of faith, and that claim is grounded in what Paul believed was the reality above all else: God loves us—forever—in Jesus Christ!

This faith sustains us when disasters happen: personal losses, deep griefs, and profound sadnesses. Through death and loss, we persist—and continue to believe—in faith. Jesus's death was followed by his resurrection, by the power of God. Through our doubts and all they bring, we can trust that our lives are held secure. For nothing will separate us from the love of Christ (Rom. 8:35). As Bavinck wrote, "The Christian, who has experienced the love of God in the forgiveness of his sins and the salvation of his soul, boasts with the apostle Paul that no tribulation or distress or persecution, no hunger or danger or sword, shall separate him from that love." We live in the deepest confidence that no matter what happens, God's deep and sustaining love holds us forever!

**Prayer Point:** Pray for a strong sense of God's love to sustain you through all your life—in times when things go well and in times of great need. Thank God for the everlasting love that ever holds you.

# 82.

# Hope Sustains and Guides

*Blessed be the God and Father of our Lord Jesus
Christ! By his great mercy he has given us a new birth
into a living hope through the resurrection of Jesus
Christ from the dead and into an inheritance that is
imperishable, undefiled, and unfading. . . . Therefore
. . . set all your hope on the grace that Jesus Christ will
bring you when he is revealed. (1 Peter 1:3–4, 13)*

I T CAN BE easy to give in to a sense of hopelessness. People
have many reasons to feel that hope is elusive. Much of what
surrounds us can cut the nerve of any hope we try to generate.

Taking a look at the world's problems—crises in nature, crises
among nations, crises for individuals in their daily lives and in
our own lives—these difficulties can seem to be intractable and
insurmountable. Hope fades, if it even exists at all.

Our Christian faith has much to say about hope. The Old
and New Testaments provide windows of hope that encourage
the people of God.

Bavinck spoke of the new life in Jesus Christ "by which a
person is inwardly changed and renewed" and said that "the
content of the new life is hope. The lives of believers are totally
sustained and guided by hope. Hope characterizes their whole

lifestyle." Bavinck notes 1 Peter 1, which begins by saying that God has "given us a new birth into a living hope through the resurrection of Jesus Christ from the dead" (1 Peter 1:3). It includes the instruction to "set all your hope on the grace that Jesus Christ will bring you when he is revealed" (1:13).

In the resurrection of Jesus Christ, the future of the world and our own futures are secured. Our lives can be a "living hope" because we know history will end with the reign of God as "King of kings and Lord of lords" (Rev. 19:16). A "new heaven and a new earth" (Rev. 21:1) will become realities.

On our way to the future, we have a "living hope" now. Hope sustains and guides us. Day by day, the realities of new life in Jesus Christ keep us going and lead us in God's ways. Hope is our lifestyle. Even when surrounding events and our own personal struggles seem to be our defining realities, we can look beyond them. We believe that God is at work, that we can serve God, and that we have a destiny to dream about—in Jesus Christ!

**Reflection Point:** Reflect on the variety of ways your faith brings you hope every day.

# 83.

# Eternal Life

*Father, the hour has come; glorify your Son so that
the Son may glorify you, since you have given him
authority over all people, to give eternal life to all
whom you have given him. And this is eternal life,
that they may know you, the only true God, and
Jesus Christ, whom you have sent. (John 17:1–3)*

JOHN 3:16 IS the most famous verse in the Bible: "For God so
loved the world that he gave his only Son, so that everyone who
believes in him may not perish but may have eternal life." This is
a central message of Scripture: God loves the world; God gave
Jesus Christ; all who believe in him have eternal life. Those are the
basics of Christian faith that we deeply believe and deeply cherish.

When it comes to the "eternal life" part of the verse, we need
to be sure we understand its meaning.

*Eternal life* usually brings to mind images of life that lasts
forever: "everlasting life." Life that is eternal has no end. Scripture promises that believing in Jesus Christ brings life that lasts
forever—eternal life lived in the presence of God and all the
saints (Rev. 7:9; 19:1, 6).

This is all true. Life after death in the presence of God is
everlasting. But there is more.

217

For Jesus, *eternal life* is something that begins now, in the present. It is a quality or kind of life. This life is life now, in the presence of God in Jesus Christ. Jesus said, "Whoever believes in the Son has eternal life" (John 3:36). Bavinck wrote that "this is the experience of the children of God . . . because God himself gave himself to them to enjoy in the Son of his love. Christ also says that eternal life for human beings, the whole of salvation, consists in the knowledge of the one and only true God and of Jesus Christ, whom he has sent." Eternal life begins now. It begins with faith in Jesus Christ, God's Son, whom God gave to die for us. United to the Son by faith, we have eternal life— now and forever. For, as Bavinck noted, "eternal life consists of nothing else than the knowledge of the one, true God in the face of Jesus Christ, the Sent One (John 17:1–3)."

Eternal life is our destiny. And eternal life starts now— through faith in Jesus Christ!

**Prayer Point:** Praise and thank God for eternal life—for life lived forever and for the "eternal" quality of life here and now when we know Jesus Christ as our Lord and Savior.

# Salvation

*There was actually no fellowship between Christ and us but only separation and opposition. For he was the only begotten and beloved Son of the Father, and we were all like the prodigal son. He was righteous and holy and without sin, and we were sinners, guilty before God and unclean from head to foot. Nevertheless, Christ has communed with us—not only in the physical sense, by taking on our nature, our flesh and blood, but also in the juridical and ethical sense, by entering into communion with our sin and death. He stands in our place; he puts himself in that relation to the law of God in which we stood to it; he takes upon himself our guilt, our sickness, our pain, our punishment; he, who knew no sin, is made sin for us, that we might be made the righteousness of God in him (2 Cor. 5:21). He became a curse for us, that he might redeem us from the curse of the law. He died for all, that they who live should no longer live for themselves but for him who died and rose again for them (2 Cor. 5:15).*

# 84.

# King of Kings

> *I charge you to keep the commandment without*
> *spot or blame until the manifestation of our Lord*
> *Jesus Christ, which he will bring about at the right*
> *time—he who is the blessed and only Sovereign, the*
> *King of kings and Lord of lords. It is he alone who*
> *has immortality and dwells in unapproachable light,*
> *whom no one has ever seen or can see; to him be honor*
> *and eternal dominion. Amen. (1 Tim. 6:13–16)*

S OMETIMES WE LOOK beyond the day-to-day difficulties of the world. There are many of these. If we lift our gaze higher, we wonder how it will all turn out. What will be the final future of the world—and the world's people, including us?

The Bible lifts us to an ultimate vision of the end of history. The big story of the Bible is that God reigns. God reigns now, in the midst of our history, and God reigns in the future, at the end of history. Regal images of God point to this reality. As Bavinck wrote, "God rules; he is the King of kings and the Lord of lords (1 Tim. 6:15; Rev. 19:6), and his kingdom lasts forever (1 Tim. 1:17)." This is the amazing—and absolutely wonderful—revelation of the world's future in God. We cannot imagine a greater vision and hope. God reigns, God rules, God's kingdom is everlasting!

This vision energizes us and pulls us ahead into the future. It means that despite all the difficulties of our days—worldwide and personal—God is at work. We are on our way to the future— the future where the fullness of God's reign will be a reality. So Bavinck says, "Neither chance nor fate, neither arbitrariness nor constraint, neither capricious whim nor iron necessity, govern nature and history, the life and fate of mankind's children. But behind all secondary causes lies and works the almighty will of an all-powerful God and a faithful Father."

To realize God rules over and in nature and history motivates us to be deeply involved wherever we can obey God's will and serve Jesus Christ. To realize our lives are held in God's providence—of which this government of God is a part—gives us the assurance and security we need to trust God's will and ways for us as we serve God. The Lord God is almighty, and the Lord God loves us as our divine Parent!

**Prayer Point:** Ask God to help the vision of God's future to shape your attitudes and actions in the present.

# Notes

Page numbers appear in chronological order, regardless of the order cited in the text. Unless otherwise indicated, quoted works are from Herman Bavinck.

**1. Theology Leads to Adoration and Worship.** *Reformed Dogmatics*, trans. John Vriend, ed. John Bolt (Grand Rapids: Baker Academic Books, 2003–8), 2:29.

**2. Faith in Christ and Scripture.** John Calvin, *Institutes of the Christian Religion*, trans. Ford Lewis Battles, ed. John T. McNeill, The Library of Christian Classics (Philadelphia: Westminster Press, 1960), 3.2.6. *Reformed Dogmatics*, 1:569.

**3. The Spirit Bears Witness.** *Reformed Dogmatics*, 1:579–80.

**4. Certainty Flows from Faith.** *The Certainty of Faith*, trans. Harry der Nederlanden (St. Catharines, ON: Paideia Press, 1980), 85–87.

**5. Center and Periphery of Scripture.** *Reformed Dogmatics*, 1:435, 439, 443–44.

❖ **Special Revelation.** *Magnalia Dei: Instruction in the Christian Religion after the Reformed Confession* (Kampen, Netherlands: J. H. Kok, 1909), 182–83. Quotations from this source have been lightly edited.

**6. The Heart and Core of Our Confession.** *Magnalia Dei*, 95, 107. Reginald Heber, "Holy, Holy, Holy," 1826.

❖ **The Divine Trinity.** *Magnalia Dei*, 106.

**7. The Fountain of All Good.** *Magnalia Dei*, 88.

**8. God's Covenant of Grace.** *Magnalia Dei*, 189–90, 197, 245, 288.

**9. God Alone Saves.** *The Philosophy of Revelation* (New York: Longmans, Green, and Co., 1909), 228.

**10. The Counsel of God.** *Magnalia Dei*, 108, 185–86.

**11. Election.** *Magnalia Dei*, 184.

**12. Christian Faith Is Pure Grace.** *Magnalia Dei*, 188.

**13. The Purpose of All World History.** "The Kingdom of God, The Highest Good," trans. Nelson D. Kloosterman, *The Bavinck Review* 2 (2011): 163.

**14. Christ Is the Turning Point of Time.** *Magnalia Dei*, 59.

**15. The Wonderful Works of God.** *Magnalia Dei*, 2. The Latin phrase *Magnalia Dei* translates to "wonderful works of God."

**16. Creation Rests on God's Good Pleasure.** *Magnalia Dei*, 112.

**17. God Maintains Creation.** *Magnalia Dei*, 119. Henry Hallam Tweedy, "Eternal God, Whose Power Upholds," 1929.

**18. Faith in God's Providence.** *Reformed Dogmatics*, 2:618–19.

❖ **Divine Providence.** *Magnalia Dei*, 122.

**19. Created in the Image of God.** *Reformed Dogmatics*, 2:530–31. *Magnalia Dei*, 139.

**20. Humans *Are* the Image of God.** *Reformed Dogmatics*, 2:554. Emphases original.

**21. Original Sin.** *Magnalia Dei*, 169.

**22. Sin Affects the Whole Person.** *Reformed Dogmatics*, 3:119. *Magnalia Dei*, 172.

**23. Idolatry.** *Magnalia Dei*, 32.

**24. Seeds of All Wickedness.** *Magnalia Dei*, 171–72.

**25. Trinitarian Salvation.** *Reformed Dogmatics*, 2:319. *Magnalia Dei*, 189.

**26. God Appears to Our Eyes.** "The Kingdom of God, The Highest Good," 147.

❖ **Jesus Christ.** *Magnalia Dei*, 196.

**27. The Incarnation, a Wonderful Confession.** *Magnalia Dei*, 224, 228.

**28. The Mystery of the Cross.** *Magnalia Dei*, 249. Isaac Watts, "When I Survey the Wondrous Cross," 1707.

**29. The Cross Is the Hand of Peace.** *Sacrifice of Praise*, trans. John Dolfin, 2nd ed. (Grand Rapids: Louis Kregel, 1922), 65.

❖ **The Work of Christ.** *Magnalia Dei*, 231.

**30. Joyful Tidings for the Whole Creation.** "The Catholicity of Christianity and the Church," trans. John Bolt, *Calvin Theological Journal* 27 (1992): 223.

**31. Christ's Resurrection Proclaims Our Acquittal.** *Magnalia Dei*, 259. *Reformed Dogmatics*, 3:442.

❖ **Jesus Christ Is Lord.** *Magnalia Dei*, 219.

**32. He Ascended into Heaven.** *Magnalia Dei*, 261–63, 272.

❖ **Christ's Ascension.** *Magnalia Dei*, 261.

**33. The Knowledge of Faith.** *Magnalia Dei*, 13–14.

**34. True Conversion.** *Magnalia Dei*, 307–8.

**35. Justification in Christ.** *Magnalia Dei*, 216, 318–20, 322. *Reformed Dogmatics*, 3:442.

❖ **New Life in Christ.** *Magnalia Dei*, 337.

**36. Adoption.** *Magnalia Dei*, 251, 327.

**37. The Church Is All Who Are Saved.** *Reformed Dogmatics*, 4:300–301.

**38. Perseverance of the Saints.** *Magnalia Dei*, 355–57.

❖ **Sanctification through Christ.** *Magnalia Dei*, 335.

**39. The Savior and Judge of the Church.** *Magnalia Dei*, 394.

**40. The Book of Life.** "Death," *The International Standard Bible Encyclopedia*, ed. James Orr et. al. (Chicago: The Howard-Severance Company, 1915), 2:812–13. P. P. Bliss, "Wonderful Words of Life," 1874.

**41. Every Knee Shall Bow.** *Sacrifice of Praise*, 120–21. *Magnalia Dei*, 399.

**42. God Is All in All.** *Magnalia Dei*, 59.

**43. One Continuous Coming of Christ.** *Magnalia Dei*, 390, 394.

**44. Amen! to All God's Promises.** *Magnalia Dei*, 360.

**45. The Comfort of Election.** *Magnalia Dei*, 185–86.

**46. Salvation Is All of Grace.** *Reformed Dogmatics*, 3:579.

❖ **Righteousness through Christ.** *Magnalia Dei*, 318.

**47. God Actually Forgives Our Sins.** *Magnalia Dei*, 186.

**48. Forgiveness Is Erasing.** *Magnalia Dei*, 250.

**49. Forgiveness Is Received by Faith.** *Magnalia Dei*, 53.

**50. Forgive Us as We Forgive.** *Magnalia Dei*, 326. William Barclay, *Gospel of Matthew*, Daily Study Bible (repr., Edinburgh: Saint Andrew Press, 1965), 1:223.

**51. A Personal Trust of the Heart.** *Magnalia Dei*, 303, 359.

**52. Being Forgiven Day by Day.** *Magnalia Dei*, 326.

**53. A Seed in the Heart.** *Magnalia Dei*, 300.

**54. We Receive the Holy Spirit.** *Reformed Ethics: Created, Fallen, and Converted Humanity*, ed. John Bolt (Grand Rapids: Baker Academic Books, 2019), 395.

❖ **The Holy Spirit in Us.** *Magnalia Dei*, 360.

**55. Sealed with the Spirit.** *Magnalia Dei*, 360–61.

**56. An Incalculable Wealth of Blessings.** *Magnalia Dei*, 282.

**57. Our Meat and Drink.** *Sacrifice of Praise*, 38.

**58. Confessing Jesus Christ.** *Sacrifice of Praise*, 48–49.

**59. The Unbreakable Unity of the Church.** *Magnalia Dei*, 368.

❖ **The Church.** *Magnalia Dei*, 361–62.

**60. Benefits of Baptism.** *Magnalia Dei*, 382. *Reformed Dogmatics*, 4:287.

**61. Members of His Body at the Lord's Supper.** *Sacrifice of Praise*, 56.

**62. The Communion and Fellowship of Christ.** *Sacrifice of Praise*, 57.

**63. Confessing Guilt.** *Sacrifice of Praise*, 61.

**64. Hearty Repentance.** *Sacrifice of Praise*, 62.

❖ **Repentance.** *Magnalia Dei*, 306.

**65. Dying and Rising.** *Magnalia Dei*, 308.

**66. Saving Faith.** *Magnalia Dei*, 304.

❖ **Mystical Union with Christ.** *Sacrifice of Praise*, 24.

**67. Cooperating with God's Purposes.** *Magnalia Dei*, 122.

**68. The Foundation of Spiritual Life.** *Reformed Ethics: Created, Fallen, and Converted Humanity*, 248.

**69. The Essence of Spiritual Life.** *Reformed Ethics: Created, Fallen, and Converted Humanity*, 248.

**70. Imitate Christ.** *Reformed Ethics: Created, Fallen, and Converted Humanity*, 339.

**71. Test and Thermometer.** *Reformed Ethics: Created, Fallen, and Converted Humanity*, 482. See also 466–81.

**72. Comfort by God Leads to Good Works.** *Magnalia Dei*, 340.

❖ **God Arouses Us to Walk in Good Works.** *Magnalia Dei*, 356.

**73. Confessing through Service.** *Sacrifice of Praise*, 58.

**74. Love for God.** *Reformed Ethics: The Duties of the Christian Life*, ed. John Bolt (Grand Rapids: Baker Academic Books, 2021), 151–53. Emphasis original.

**75. The Spirit of Love in the Law.** *Magnalia Dei*, 53.

**76. Continuing Christ's Compassion.** *Reformed Ethics: The Duties of the Christian Life*, 444, 446.

**77. Live the Life of Love.** *Magnalia Dei*, 370.

**78. Neighbor Love to Everyone.** *Reformed Ethics: The Duties of the Christian Life*, 424–27.

**79. Love for Neighbor.** *Magnalia Dei*, 8.

**80. The Value of the Whole World.** *The Philosophy of Revelation*, 270.

**81. Nothing Separates Us from God's Love.** *Magnalia Dei*, 122.

**82. Hope Sustains and Guides.** *Reformed Dogmatics*, 4:49–50, 52.

**83. Eternal Life.** *Magnalia Dei*, 10.

❖ **Salvation.** *Magnalia Dei*, 249.

**84. King of Kings.** *Magnalia Dei*, 122.

# Selected Herman Bavinck Resources in English

*The Certainty of Faith*. Trans. Harry der Nederlanden. St. Catharines, ON: Paideia Press, 1980. https://www.monergism.com/certainty-faith.

*Herman Bavinck on Preaching and Preachers*. Ed. and trans. James P. Eglinton. Peabody, MA: Hendricksen Publishers, 2017.

*Magnalia Dei: Instruction in the Christian Religion after the Reformed Confession*. Kampen, Netherlands: J. H. Kok, 1909. https://archive.org/details/magnalia-dei-bavinck-english.

*On Theology: Herman Bavinck's Academic Orations*. Ed. and trans. Bruce R. Pass. Boston: Brill, 2021.

*Our Reasonable Faith: A Survey of Christian Doctrine*. Trans. Henry Zylstra. 1956. Reprint, Grand Rapids: Baker Book House, 1977.

*The Philosophy of Revelation*. New York: Longmans, Green, and Co., 1909.

*Reformed Dogmatics*. Trans. John Vriend. Ed. John Bolt. 4 vols. Grand Rapids: Baker Academic Books, 2003–8.

*Reformed Dogmatics: Abridged in One Volume*. Ed. John Bolt. Grand Rapids: Baker Academic Books, 2011.

*Reformed Ethics: Created, Fallen, and Converted Humanity*. Ed. John Bolt. Grand Rapids: Baker Academic Books, 2019.

*Reformed Ethics: The Duties of the Christian Life*. Ed. John Bolt. Grand Rapids: Baker Academic Books, 2021.

*The Sacrifice of Praise.* Trans. John Dolfin. 2nd ed. Grand Rapids: Louis Kregel, 1922. https://archive.org/details /sacrificeofprais00bavi/page/n6/mode/2up.

*The Wonderful Works of God.* Trans. Henry Zylstra. 1956. Reprint, Glenside, PA: Westminster Seminary Press, 2020.

# Selected Resources
# for Further Reflection

Bolt, John. *Bavinck on the Christian Life: Following Jesus in Faithful Service*. Wheaton: Crossway, 2015.

———. *A Theological Analysis of Herman Bavinck's Two Essays on the Imitatio Christi: Between Pietism and Modernism*. Lewiston, NY: Edwin Mellen Press, 2013.

Bremmer, R. H. "Bavinck, Herman." *Encyclopedia of the Reformed Faith*. Ed. Donald K. McKim. Louisville, KY: Westminster John Knox Press, 1992.

Brock, Cory C. *Orthodox Yet Modern: Herman Bavinck's Use of Friedrich Schleiermacher*. Bellingham, WA: Lexham Press, 2020.

Eglinton, James. *Bavinck: A Critical Biography*. Grand Rapids: Baker Academic Books, 2020.

———. "Everybody Loves Bavinck: How a Dutch Neo-Calvinist Thinker Became the Latest Christian Theologian-Du-Jour." *Christianity Today*, February 18, 2022, https://www.christianitytoday.com/ct/2022/february-web-only/herman-bavinck-dutch-calvinist-theologian.html.

———. *Trinity and Organism: Towards a New Reading of Herman Bavinck's Organic Motif*. London: Bloomsbury T&T Clark, 2012.

Gleason, Ron. *Herman Bavinck: Pastor, Churchman, Statesman, and Theologian*. Phillipsburg, NJ: P&R, 2010.

Pass, Bruce R. *The Heart of Dogmatics: Christology and Christocentrism in Herman Bavinck*. Göttingen, Germany: Vandenhock & Ruprecht, 2020.

Rogers, Jack B., and Donald K. McKim. *The Authority and Interpretation of the Bible: An Historical Approach*. San Francisco: Harper & Row, 1979.

Sutanto, Nathaniel Gray. *God and Knowledge: Herman Bavinck's Theological Epistemology*. New York: T&T Clark, 2020.